Doggin' Je

The 100 Best Places To Hike With Your Dog In The Garden State

DOUG GELBERT

illustrations by

ANDREW CHESWORTH

Cruden Bay Books

There is always a new trail to look forward to...

DOGGIN' JERSEY: THE 100 BEST PLACES TO HIKE WITH
YOUR DOG IN THE GARDEN STATE

Cruden Bay Books
PO Box 467
Montchanin, DE 19710
www.hikewithyourdog.com

International Standard Book Number 0-9785622-2-4

*"Dogs are our link to paradise...to sit with a dog on a hillside
on a glorious afternoon is to be back in Eden,
where doing nothing was not boring - it was peace."*
- Milan Kundera

Ahead On The Trail

Introduction

New Jersey can be a great place to hike with your dog. Within an hour or so drive from most anywhere in the state you can hike on sand trails, climb mountains that leave your dog panting, walk on some of the most historic grounds in America, explore the estates of America's wealthiest families or circle lakes for miles and never lose sight of the water.

I have selected what I consider to be the 100 best places to take your dog for an outing and ranked them according to subjective criteria including the variety of hikes available, opportunities for canine swimming and pleasure of the walks. The rankings include a mix of parks that feature long walks and parks that contain short walks. Did I miss your favorite? Let us know at *www.hikewithyourdog.com*.

For dog owners it is important to realize that not all parks are open to our best trail companions (see page 14 for a list of parks that do not allow dogs). It is sometimes hard to believe but not everyone loves dogs. We are, in fact, in the minority when compared with our non-dog owning neighbors.

So when visiting a park always keep your dog under control and clean up any messes and we can all expect our great parks to remain open to our dogs. And maybe some others will see the light as well. Remember, every time you go out with your dog you are an ambassador for all dog owners.

Grab that leash and hit the trail!
DBG

Hiking with Your Dog

So you want to start hiking with your dog. Hiking with your dog can be a fascinating way to explore New Jersey from a canine perspective. Some things to consider:

🐾 Dog's Health
Hiking can be a wonderful preventative for any number of physical and behavioral disorders. One in every three dogs is overweight and running up trails and leaping through streams is great exercise to help keep pounds off. Hiking can also relieve boredom in a dog's routine and calm dogs prone to destructive habits. And hiking with your dog strengthens the overall owner/dog bond.

🐾 Breed of Dog
All dogs enjoy the new scents and sights of a trail. But some dogs are better suited to hiking than others. If you don't as yet have a hiking companion, select a breed that matches your interests. Do you look forward to an entire afternoon's hiking? You'll need a dog bred to keep up with such a pace, such as a retriever or a spaniel. Is a half-hour enough walking for you? It may not be for an energetic dog like a border collie. If you already have a hiking friend, tailor your plans to his abilities.

🐾 Conditioning
Just like humans, dogs need to be acclimated to the task at hand. An inactive dog cannot be expected to bounce from the easy chair in the den to complete a 3-hour hike. You must also be physically able to restrain your dog if confronted with distractions on the trail (like a scampering squirrel or a pack of joggers). Have your dog checked by a veterinarian before significantly increasing his activity level.

🐾 Weather
Hot humid summers do not do dogs any favors. With no sweat glands and only panting available to disperse body heat, dogs are much more susceptible to heat stroke than we are. Unusually rapid panting and/or a bright red tongue are signs of heat exhaustion in your pet.

Always carry enough water for your hike. Even days that don't seem too warm can cause discomfort in dark-coated dogs if the sun is shining brightly. In cold weather, short-coated breeds may require additional attention.

🐾 Trail Hazards

Dogs won't get poison ivy but they can transfer it to you. Stinging nettle is a nuisance plant that lurks on the side of many trails and the slightest brush will deliver troublesome needles into a dog's coat. Some trails are littered with small pieces of broken glass that can slice a dog's paws. Nasty thorns can also blanket trails that we in shoes may never notice.

🐾 Ticks

You won't be able to visit any of New Jersey's parks without encountering ticks. All are nasty but the deer tick - no bigger than a pin head - carries with it the spectre of Lyme disease. Lyme disease attacks a dog's joints and makes walking painful. The tick needs to be embedded in the skin to transmit Lyme disease. It takes 4-6 hours for a tick to become embedded and another 24-48 hours to transmit Lyme disease bacteria.

When hiking, walk in the middle of trails away from tall grass and bushes. And when the summer sun fades away don't stop thinking about ticks - they remain active any time the temperature is above 30 degrees. By checking your dog - and yourself - thoroughly after each walk you can help avoid Lyme disease. Ticks tend to congregate on your dog's ears, between the toes and around the neck and head.

🐾 Water

Surface water, including fast-flowing streams, is likely to be infested with a microscopic protozoa called *Giardia*, waiting to wreak havoc on a dog's intestinal system. The most common symptom is crippling diarrhea. Algae, pollutants and contaminants can all be in streams, ponds and puddles. If possible, carry fresh water for your dog on the trail - your dog can even learn to drink happily from a squirt bottle.

Rattlesnakes

Rattlesnakes are not particularly aggressive animals but you should treat any venomous snake with respect and keep your distance. A rattler's colors may vary but they are recognized by the namesake rattle on the tail and a diamond-shaped head. Unless cornered or teased by humans or dogs, a rattlesnake will crawl away and avoid striking. Avoid placing your hand in unexamined rocky areas and crevasses and try and keep your dog from doing so as well. If you hear a nearby rattle, stop immediately and hold your dog back. Identify where the snake is and slowly back away.

If you or your dog is bitten, do not panic but get to a hospital or veterinarian with as little physical movement as possible. Wrap between the bite and the heart. Rattlesnakes might give "dry bites" where no poison is injected, but you should always check with a doctor after a bite even if you feel fine.

Black Bears

Are you likely to see a bear while out hiking with your dog? No, it's not likely. it is, however, quite a thrill if you are fortunate enough to spot a black bear on the trail - from a distance.

Black bear attacks are incredibly rare. In the year 2000 a hiker was killed by a black bear in Great Smoky National Park and it was the first deadly bear attack in the 66-year history of America's most popular national park. It was the first EVER in the southeastern United States. In all of North America only 43 black bear mauling deaths have ever been recorded (through 1999).

Most problems with black bears occur near a campground (like the above incident) where bears have learned to forage for unprotected food. On the trail bears will typically see you and leave the area. What should you do if you encounter a black bear? Experts agree on three important things:

1) Never run. A bear will outrun you, outclimb you, outswim you. Don't look like prey.
2) Never get between a female bear and a cub who may be nearby feeding.
3) Leave a bear an escape route.

If the bear is at least 15 feet away and notices you make sure you keep your dog close and calm. If a bear stands on its hind legs or comes closer it may just be trying to get a better view or smell to evaluate the situation. Wave your arms and make noise to scare the bear away. Most bears will quickly leave the area.

If you encounter a black bear at close range, stand upright and make yourself appear as large a foe as possible. Avoid direct eye contact and speak in a calm, assertive and assuring voice as you back up slowly and out of danger.

🐾 Porcupines

Porcupines are easy for a curious dog to catch and that makes them among the most dangerous animals you may meet because an embedded quill is not only painful but can cause infection if not properly removed.

Outfitting Your Dog For A Hike

These are the basics for taking your dog on a hike:

▸ **Collar.**
It should not be so loose as to come off but you should be able to slide your flat hand under the collar.

▸ **Identification Tags.**
Get one with your veterinarian's phone number as well.

▸ **Bandanna.**
Can help distinguish him from game in hunting season.

▸ **Leash.**
Leather lasts forever but if there's water in your dog"s future, consider quick-drying nylon.

▸ **Water.**
Carry 8 ounces for every hour of hiking.

🐾 *I want my dog to help carry water, snacks and other supplies on the trail. Where do I start?*
To select an appropriate dog pack measure your dog's girth around the rib cage. A dog pack should fit securely without hindering the dog's ability to walk normally.

🐾 *Will my dog wear a pack?*
Wearing a dog pack is no more obtrusive than wearing a collar, although some dogs will take to a pack easier than others. Introduce the pack by draping a towel over your dog's back in the house and then having your dog wear an empty pack on short walks. Progressively add some crumpled newspaper and then bits of clothing. Fill the pack with treats and reward your dog from the stash. Soon your dog will associate the dog pack with an outdoor adventure and will eagerly look forward to wearing it.

🐾 *How much weight can I put into a dog pack?*

Many dog packs are sold by weight recommendations. A healthy, well-conditioned dog can comfortably carry 25% to 33% of its body weight. Breeds prone to back problems or hip dysplasia should not wear dog packs. Consult your veterinarian before stuffing the pouches with gear.

🐾 *How does a dog wear a pack?*

The pack, typically with cargo pouches on either side, should ride as close to the shoulders as possible without limiting movement. The straps that hold the dog pack in place should be situated where they will not cause chafing.

🐾 *What are good things to put in a dog pack?*

Low density items such as food and poop bags are good choices. Ice cold bottles of water can cool your dog down on hot days. Don't put anything in a dog pack that can break. Dogs will bang the pack on rocks and trees as they wiggle through tight spots in the trail. Dogs also like to lie down in creeks and other wet spots so seal items in plastic bags. A good use for dog packs when on day hikes around New Jersey is trail maintenance - your dog can pack out trash left by inconsiderate visitors before you.

❧ *Are dog booties a good idea?*

Dog booties can be an asset, especially for the occasional canine hiker whose paw pads have not become toughened. Some trails around New Jersey involve rocky terrain. In some places, there may be broken glass. Hiking boots for dogs are designed to prevent pads from cracking while trotting across rough surfaces. Used in winter, dog booties provide warmth and keep ice balls from forming between toe pads when hiking through snow.

❧ *What should a doggie first aid kit include?*

Even when taking short hikes it is a good idea to have some basics available for emergencies:

▸ 4" square gauze pads
▸ cling type bandaging tapes
▸ topical wound disinfectant cream
▸ tweezers
▸ insect repellent - no reason to leave your dog unprotected against mosquitoes and blackflies
▸ veterinarian's phone number

"I can't think of anything that brings me closer to tears than when my old dog - completely exhausted after a hard day in the field - limps away from her nice spot in front of the fire and comes over to where I'm sitting and puts her head in my lap, a paw over my knee, and closes her eyes, and goes back to sleep. I don't know what I've done to deserve that kind of friend."
-Gene Hill

Low Impact Hiking With Your Dog

Every time you hike with your dog on the trail you are an ambassador for all dog owners. Some people you meet won't believe in your right to take a dog on the trail. Be friendly to all and make the best impression you can by practicing low impact hiking with your dog:

- Pack out everything you pack in.

- Do not leave dog scat on the trail; if you haven't brought plastic bags for poop removal bury it away from the trail and topical water sources.

- Hike only where dogs are allowed.

- Stay on the trail.

- Do not allow your dog to chase wildlife.

- Step off the trail and wait with your dog while horses and other hikers pass.

- Do not allow your dog to bark - people are enjoying the trail for serenity.

- *Have as much fun on your hike as your dog does.*

The Other End Of The Leash

Leash laws are like speed limits - everyone seems to have a private interpretation of their validity. Some dog owners never go outside with an unleashed dog; others treat the laws as suggestions or disregard them completely. It is not the purpose of this book to tell dog owners where to go to evade the leash laws or reveal the parks where rangers will look the other way at an unleashed dog. Nor is it the business of this book to preach vigilant adherence to the leash laws. Nothing written in a book is going to change people's behavior with regard to leash laws. So this will be the last time leash laws are mentioned, save occasionally when we point out the parks where dogs are welcomed off leash.

How To Pet A Dog
Tickling tummies slowly and gently works wonders.
Never use a rubbing motion; this makes dogs bad-tempered.
A gentle tickle with the tips of the fingers is all that is necessary
to induce calm in a dog. I hate strangers who go up to dogs with their
hands held to the dog's nose, usually palm towards themselves.
How does the dog know that the hand doesn't hold something horrid?
The palm should always be shown to the dog and go straight
down to between the dog's front legs and tickle gently with
a soothing voice to acompany the action.
Very often the dog raises its back leg in a scratching movement,
it gets so much pleasure from this.
-Barbara Woodhouse

No Dogs

Before we get started on the best places to take your dog, let's get out of the way the trails that do not allow dogs:

Bergen County
Flat Rock Brook Nature Center
Monument Park
Tenafly Nature Center

Burlington County
Rancocas Nature Center

Camden County
Palmyra Cove Nature Park

Cape May County
Cape May County Park
Cape May Migratory Bird Refuge
Cape May State Park - trails

Gloucester County
Ceres Park
Greenwich Lake Park
Red Bank Battlefield Park
Scotland Run Park
Washington Lake Park

Middlesex County
Plainsboro Preserve

Monmouth County
Deep Cut Arboretum

Morris County
Bamboo Brook Education Center
Great Swamp National Wildlife Refuge
Willowwood Arboretum

Ocean County
Forsythe NWR - Holgate

Passaic County
Weis Ecology Center

Somerset County
Lord Stirling Park

Sussex County
Wallkill River National Wildlife Refuge

Warren County
Johnsonburg Swamp
Pequest Wildlife Management Area

O.K. that wasn't too bad. Let's forget about these and move on to some of the great places where we CAN take our dogs across New Jersey...

The Best of the Best

1. Stokes State Forest
What are you looking for on an outing with your dog - a variety of short, peaceful hikes? A strenuous, multi-hour trek that will have your dog sleeping the whole ride home? Memorable views? Lakes? Rushing streams? Stokes has it all.

2. Wills Mills County Park
You say you want to experience the great Pine Barrens but don't want to lose yourself with your dog on miles of unmapped, unmarked sand roads? This park will get you into the pinelands on paw-friendly trails through diverse habitats and, yes, throw in a bit of elevation change along the way.

3. Pyramid Mountain Natural Historic Area
If this park just offered the interesting sights on the Pyramid Mountain trails it would be enough to get highly ranked but there's a whole other trail system across the road!

4. Delaware Water Gap National Recreation Area
The hike up Mount Tammany leads to the most famous view in New Jersey but coming down your dog will love the waterfalls in Dunnfield Creek even more. If you come when the moutain laurel is in full bloom you will truly find yourself on one of the best canine hikes in New Jersey.

5. Norvin Green State Forest
There are plenty of places in northern New Jersey to disappear into the mountains with your dog but Norvin Green stands out with its variety of summits and a couple of waterfalls and played-out mines for flavor.

6. Clayton Park

For no-frills canine hiking where you just jump out of the car and into a natural, uncrowded woodland with your dog it is hard to top this Monmouth County park.

7. Worthington State Forest

Long canine hikes are on the menu here, studded with star destinations: Sunfish Pond, the Appalachian Trail, Rattlesnake Swamp, Van Campens Glen, Coppermines....

8. Wharton State Forest

What dog won't love these flat, paw-friendly, packed-sand hiking surfaces in the Pine Barrens? And there are 500 miles of them! Pure, tea-colored streams percolate up through the sandy soil for excellent doggie swimming pools.

9. Island Beach State Park

You can bring your dog here to swim in the ocean in the middle of the summer. Nuff said!

10. Parvin State Park

The premier place to bring your dog for a hike in South Jersey. No hills and no views but your dog won't be complaining and won't be able to wipe the wag off her tail on these paw-friendly wooded trails. parvin Lake is a great spot for your dog to jump in as well.

"What counts is not necessarily the size of the dog in the fight but the size of the fight in the dog."
-Dwight D. Eisenhower

The 100 Best Places To Hike With Your Dog In New Jersey...

1
Stokes
State Forest

The Park

The State of New Jersey began buying land for Stokes Forest in 1907 - sometimes paying a whole dollar an acre. The forest is named for Edward Casper Stokes who served one term as Republican governor from 1905 until 1908, forming the New Jersey Forest Commission during his tenure. He donated the first 500 acres.

After he left office Stokes remained active in politics, failing in three bids to win a U.S. Senate seat and another term as governor. In 2001, lightning struck his mausoleum in the Mount Pleasant Cemetery in Millville. The lightning blasted through the mausoleum's roof and littered the floor with shattered marble, blowing a 6-inch hole in the governor's crypt. His casket was not damaged.

Sussex

Phone Number
- (973) 948-3820

Website
- www.nj.gov/dep/parksandfor-ests/parks/stokes.html

Admission Fee
- Charged in the summer in the recreation areas

Directions
- Take Route 206 north of Branchville for four miles to the park office on the right.

The Walks

Stokes Forest is the chunk of land between the Delaware Water Gap National Recreation Area to the south and High Point State Park to the north giving New Jersey about 30 miles of uninterrupted parkland along the Kittatinny Ridge of the Appalachian Mountains. Lodged between two more celebrated neighbors, Stokes can sometimes get overlooked. With 25 named trails, that should never happen for canine hikers.

Any type of canine hike is possible here - you could fill up a day just walking on beginner-to-moderate type trails that explore attractive streams, visit old mine sites or just disappear with your dog in a remote patch of woodsland. But most visitors will point their dogs in the direction of Kittatinny Ridge and 1,653-foot Sunrise Mountain. Four trails lead to the *Appalachian Trail* atop the ridge in the vicinity of Sunrise Mountain enabling you to create hiking loops of between four and ten miles, depending on how long you want to walk on the ridge soaking in the views. This is absolutely a workout for your dog and the terrain can be rocky - take care especially coming down across large slabs of stone.

Your dog will stop often for the long views from Sunrise Mountain.

To cap off your dog's day at Stokes Forest head to Tillman Ravine for easy walking through a dark, shady evergreen forest of eastern hemlock. The Tillman Brook that carves this moist ravine is one of the prettiest in the state.

Trail Sense: The best trail guide in New Jersey can be had at the office and the markings are regularly attended to out on the trails.

Dog Friendliness
Dogs are permitted on all Stokes trails but not in the campgrounds.
Traffic
Even at its busiest you won't feel crowded on these trails.
Canine Swimming
There is no water along the Kittatinny Ridge but plenty of opportunity for a refreshing swim through the valley.
Trail Time
As much as a full day of canine hiking.

2
Wells Mills
County Park

The Park

The last royal sheriff of Monmouth County, Elisha Lawrence was put in command of the British New Jersey Volunteers on July 1, 1776. A year later, in skirmishing on Staten Island, Lieutenant-Colonel Lawrence was captured. He subsequently took refuge in Nova Scotia before returning to Britain where he died in Wales.

His extensive landholdings were seized and James Wells won the land that would become this county park 200 years later at auction. Wells dammed Oyster Creek to build a sawmill to process the large stands of Atlantic white cedar found here.

The Estlow family acquired the property in the late 1800s and built adjacent sawmills, hence the pluralistic park name. Possession of the land passed to the Conrads, a prominent local business family, in 1936. When the tax burden of the land became too onerous in the late 1970s the New Jersey Conservation Foundation took control, beginning the process that insured protection of this slice of Pine Barrens as a public park.

Ocean

Phone Number
- (609) 971-3085

Website
- http://www.ocean.nj.us/parks/wellsmills.html

Admission Fee
- None

Directions
- The park is on Route 532, west of the Garden State Parkway. Northbound, take Exit 69 and make a left going west on Route 532. Southbound, use Exit 67 onto Route 554 West and continue to Route 72. Make a right and another right on Route 532 to the park entrance on the right.

The Walks

The queen of Ocean County parks at over 900 acres, Wells Mills is also on the top of any list for canine hikers. The trails trip through a rich variety of habitat from cedar swamps to thick pine-oak woodlands. Most of the going is on paw-friendly sand or soft dirt covered in pine straw.

But what truly sets Wells Mills apart from its Pine Barrens neighbors is elevation change. Nothing grueling but in the western part of the park the

22

trails roll joyously up and down across small ridges and sandhills. The namesake mound of sand on the *Penns Hill Trail*, the longest of the park's routes at 8.4 miles, reaches 126 feet. That white-blazed trail circles the perimeter of the park; a simliar shorter route is the green-blazed *Estlow Trail* at 3.5 miles.

Additional loops up to 1.3 miles can be hiked near the Nature Center. All told Wells Mills maintains more than 16 miles of trails.

Trail Sense: The trails are energetically blazed, an excellent trail map is available and a detailed mapboard is at the parking lot. The trails are also meticulously measured, down to the hundreth of a mile to help you select a suitable distance hike.

Dog Friendliness
Dogs can use all the Wells Mills trails; poop bags are available.

Traffic
This is a popular park but there is plenty of room to spread out on the trails. Bikes are restricted to the Yellow Bike Trail and motorized vehicles are prohibited.

Canine Swimming
Spurs from the Estlow Trail reach out and tickle the shore of Wells Mills Lake for a doggie dip. The crystal clear waters of Oyster Creek and Raccoon Branch are not deep enough for more than a splash.

Trail Time
Anywhere up to a half-day.

"If there are no dogs in Heaven,
then when I die I want to go where they went."
-Anonymous

3
Pyramid Mountain Natural Historic Area

The Park

Hikers had been coming to Pyramid Mountain for decades to enjoy the wilderness but it wasn't until 1987, when the spectre of expanding suburbia raised its ugly head, that grassroots efforts led to the creation of a permanent public open space. The Pyramid Mountain Natural Historic Area now protects more than 1,500 acres of varied trails, fields, forests and wetlands.

The Walks

There is quite a menu for canine hikers at Pyramid Mountain. Looking for views? Exposed promontories will provide long looks to the mountains in the west or as far as New York City to the east. Want a waterside ramble? Check out the *Orange Trail* that works

Morris

Phone Number
- (973) 334-3130

Website
- www.morrisparks.net/parks/pyrmtnmain.htm

Admission Fee
- None

Directions
- From I-287 take Exit 45 onto Wooten Street, turning left from northbound or onto Myrtle Avenue and turning right southbound. Go up the hill to the blinking red light and turn right onto Boonton Avenue (Route 511). Proceed to the park entrance on the left after 2.5 miles.

the slopes under a rocky ridge along the Taylortown Reservoir. Like to poke around ruins? You'll find old homesteads and the remains of stone cottages along the Pyramid Mountain trails. Seeking a leafy ravine to escape to with your dog? You can do it here.

Pyramid Mountain tops out at only 924 feet and the summit can be reached mostly on soft dirt, paw-friendly trails. There are enough short, steep climbs, however, to remind your dog he is on a mountain. All told you be climbing about 300 feet.

The summit and Tripod Rock are mandatory destinations for first time visitors but don't be too quick to load the dog in the car and drive away when you get off the mountain. Across Boonton Avenue there is actually more parkland than the Pyramid Mountain side. The terrain is less flashy, mostly meat-

-and-potatoes stuff but you will find picturesque wetlands, a moderate ascent to the top of 892-foot Turkey Mountain, views of the New York skyline and long, uninterrupted stretches of easily rolling woods walking. Depending on your route - and there are many choices - you can get five miles or so of canine hiking on the east side of the park.

Tripod Rock can provide your dog some welcome shady relief after a sporty climb to the top of Pyramid Mountain.

Trail Sense: The trail system is well-marked and trail junctions are usually obvious. A detailed trail map is available outside the Visitor Center.

Dog Friendliness

Dogs are permitted to enjoy these trails.

Traffic

If you are used to hiking with your dog in some of the more remote mountain areas of New Jersey, Pyramid Mountain may seem like you have signed up for a parade on sunny weekends.

Canine Swimming

The Orange Trail drops to the lake shoreline for some excellent dog paddling and Botts Pond is a good swimming hole on the east side. There are no streams on top of Pyramid Mountain so pack plenty of liquid refreshment on a steamy afternoon.

Trail Time

Several hours to a full day.

4
Delaware Water Gap
National Recreaton Area–
Kittaninny Point

The Park

In the Lenni Lenape language Kittaninny means "endless mountain" which is quite ironic when looking at Mount Tammany where the 1,527-foot high Kittaninny Ridge ends abruptly by plunging 1200 feet into the Delaware River.

It didn't take much imagination for early American entrepreneurs to dream of glorious resorts in the vicinity of one of New Jersey's great wonders. More recently U.S. Army engineers en-visioned damming the gap and creating a giant reservoir for water supply and recreation.

Amidst great controversy the Tocks Island Dam project was finally scuttled in 1992 and today the Delaware Water Gap National Recreation Area encompasses 70,000 acres for more than 30 miles along the Delaware River on both the New Jersey and Pennsylvania sides.

Warren

Phone Number
- (570) 828-2253

Website
- http://www.nps.gov/dewa/index.htm

Admission Fee
- None for the park; fees for recreation areas where dogs are not allowed

Directions
- Traveling west on I-80 exit into the rest area as you enter the Water Gap approaching Pennsylvania. You can park in the rest area but the actual parking lot is just beyond on the right.

The Walks

The climb up Mount Tammany may be the steepest canine hike in New Jersey but not beyond the capabilities of a healthy dog. The *Red-Dot Trail* covers the 1200-foot elevation gain in 1.5 miles using switchbacks on an oft-times rocky path under paw. There is one 30-foot rock climb that will need to be negotiated.

After enjoying the spectacular views push away from the Water Gap on the *Blue-Dot Trail*. A welcome respite in light woods on the level ridge begins a long, steady descent accentuated by groves of mountain laurel in the early summer.

You will eventually reach the white-blazed *Appalachian Trail* along

Dunnfield Creek that you'll use to close this four-mile loop. You will be greeted immediately by one of the many waterfalls on the tumbling brook and this one creates a perfect doggie swimming hole at the ideal time for refreshment - the first water encountered on this strenuous hike.

Trail Sense: The hardest navigation is done at the beginning - finding the trailhead. From the main parking lot, turn and walk back towards I-80 to pick up the Red-Dot Trail.

Dog Friendliness

Dogs are not allowed in the Kittatinny Point Visitor Center and picnic area or Watergate Recreation Site in New Jersey. There isn't much point in taking your dog to any of the Pennsylvania attractions.

Traffic

The climb to the Mount Tammany and Mount Minsi summits are busy at any time of the year. On nice spring weekends the trail to the top of Mount Tammany can resemble a cattle chute.

Canine Swimming

You will need to travel up Old Mine Road to get access into the Delaware River.

Trail Time

Allow three hours to complete the circuit to the Mount Tammany summit and back.

These falls along Dunnfield Creek are the perfect place
for a dog to cool down after a spirited climb on
Mount Tammany.

5
Norvin Green State Forest

The Park

This area supported active mining through the 1800s but officials began eyeing the Wanaque River as a potential water source as far back as the 1870s. Construction on the Wanaque Dam began in 1920 and a decade - and $25 million and 70 homes - later New Jersey communities began tapping into the some 30 billion gallons of water held in Wanaque Reservoir.

The state forest is named for its donor, Norvin Hewlett Green. Most of the trails across the 4,210 acres of forest were cut by the members of the Green Mountain Club in the early 1920s.

The Walks

The attraction at Norvin Green are numerous viewpoints on hilltops ranging to 1,300 feet, most reached via some of the best, albeit rugged, canine hiking in New Jersey. There are many places to spend the day with your dog in the northern highlands and if this isn't first on your list it should be in the discussion.

The nearest destinations to the parking lot are the remainders of the mining era of the 1800s along the

Passaic

Phone Number
- (973) 835-2160
(Weis Ecology Center)

Website
- nj.gov/dep/parksandforests/
parks/norvin.html

Admission Fee
- None

Directions
- Take I-287 to Exit 57. Follow Skyline Drive to Greenwood Lake Turnpike to West Brook Road to Snake Den Road. Follow signs to Weis Ecology Center. Park in the lot before the center or along Burnt Meadow Road and Glen Wild Road.

When the bats are out your dog can go into the Roomy Mine.

Red/Yellow Trail. A short detour climbs to Roomy Mine that you can actually explore with your dog in the warmer months when bats are not hibernating.

Bring a flashlight and you can enter for 50 feet or so. Up the trail is the flooded Blue Mine that produced tons of ore before the encroaching water could not be abated in 1908.

Past the mines the climbing begins on sometimes rocky and rooty woods trails. High Point, at 960 feet far from the tallest peak in the park, rewards you with 360-degree views after a steep last ascent. If you choose to penetrate deeper into Norvin State Forest there is a Coney-Island type rollercoaster trail to Carris Hill and more views in every direction. Down the hill on the *White Trail* is the split plunge of Chikahoki Falls.

Trail Sense: There are many trails in Norvin Green State Forest, mostly in moderately-sized segments. Some use the same pathway. Without a map you would be surprised how easy it is to get mis-directed here. Before setting out stop at the Weis Ecology Center and grab one.

Dog Friendliness
Dogs are permitted in Norvin State Forest but not in the adjoining Weis Environmental Center.

Traffic
A smattering of trail users can be expected but are uncommon.

Canine Swimming
The streams on the mountainside are suitable only for splashing but a detour (or your main desitination) can lead to the shore of Wanaque Reservoir.

Trail Time
Many hours on Norvin Green's trails are possible.

Your dog will enjoy views in every direction on the bare rock summit of High Point.

13

Clayton Park

The Park

For most of the 20th century Paul Clayton shunned modern farming methods, working his fields by hand with his five horses growing potatoes, tomatoes, grains and corn until 1971 when he retired at the age of 87. For years he turned down lucrative offers to harvest the trees on his property along Doctor's Creek. Instead he sold his 176 acres to Monmouth County in 1978 for a price below market value. The county has since doubled the size of Clayton Park to its current 421 acres of hardwoods.

The Walks

Clayton Park is a true jewel for New Jersey canine hikers with about eight miles of sandy dirt paths traipsing through airy stands of towering beech, black oak and tulip poplar. The trail system is neatly divided into two stacked-loops by a wide ravine so you can bring your dog for a satisfying loop of less than one hour or carve out a longer hiking day.

You will start on the *Bridges Trail* that rolls around ridges and through valleys; the ups and downs go down easy on these well-maintained paths. If you choose a big canine hiking day you will penetrate deeper into the core of the Clayton forest on the 1.5-mile *Old Forge Trail* or finish the Bridges loop by skirting farm fields. Either way you will spend time along the wetlands of Doctor's Creek that will eventually drain in the Delaware River.

Trail Sense: A trail map is available at the trailhead.

Monmouth

Phone Number
- None

Website
- www.monmouthcountyparks.com/parks/claytonpark.asp

Admission Fee
- No

Directions
- From I-195 Take Exit 11 (Imlaystown/Cox's Corner) and head south on Route 43 that will soon reach Route 526. Turn left and make an immediate right on Davis Station Road (there is a small park sign). Go through the village and after one mile make a left onto Emley's Hill Road and follow to the parking lot on the left.

Dog Friendliness
Dogs are welcome and poop bags are provided.

Traffic
The trails are open to mountain bikes and horses but don't expect much competition for these wonderful trails.

Canine Swimming
Doctor's Creek is too marshy for a good swim but there is a small farm pond along the Bridges Trail that will support dog paddling.

Trail Time
More than one hour.

7
Worthington State Forest

The Park

The Dutch used Old Mine Road to transport minerals up through the Hudson River Valley in the 1600s, laying the foundation for the claim that it is the oldest commercial road in North America.

In 1903, Charles C. Worthington, President of the Worthington Pump Company, laid plans for his own transportation system. He would build a pipeline to bring water down from Sunfish Pond at the top of Kittatinny Ridge to his farm on Shawnee Island.

Worthington owned more than 8,000 acres of land around the mountain. He fenced in the property with an eleven-mile fence and imported whitetail deer from Virginia to replace deer that had become extinct in New Jersey. When he tore down the fence, the roaming deer became the ancestors of deer herds across the state.

After his death Worthington's sons operated his diverse business interests until 1954 when the State of New Jersey acquired the first parcels of land that would become the 6,000-acre Worthington State Forest.

Warren

Phone Number
- (908) 841-9575

Website
- http://www.nj.gov/dep/park-sandforests/parks/worthington.html

Admission Fee
- None

Directions
- Take I-80 West to the last exit in New Jersey (Millbrook/Flatbrookville), getting in the right lane as the higway bends right. At the bottom of the ramp, turn right onto Old Mine Road. The park office is three miles on the left.

The Walks

Trailheads for a potpouri of canine hiking spring up along Old Mine Road. The first you come to is the *Karanac Trail*, an easy canine hike to the sandy shores of the Delaware River. Next come a series of trails that lead to the top of the mountain starting with the *Douglas Trail* that climbs 980 feet to Sunfish Pond in two miles. The blue-blazed path is named for Supreme Court Justice William O. Douglas who participated in a protest hike in 1967 over management practices proposed for the glacial pond.

Sunfish Pond is certainly worth a good long look.

Another hike to the *Appalachian Trail* at the top of the mountain is the *Coppermines Trail* that passes two ancient open-faced mines before meandering up the slopes. Once on top of the mountains a 5-mile loop to Rattlesnake Swamp is possible - be careful as you cross to the eastern edge of the ridge as your dog will be walking on exposed cliff faces.

Farther up the road you reach Van Campens Glen and an out-and-back trail leading to a sparkling waterfall in about 30 minutes. This is a fine choice for a hot day as your dog will stay cool hiking in the shady ravine and beside the roiling brook. Finally at the end of Old Mine Road you reach the preserved Millbrook Village where your dog can trot down an old logging road.

Trail Sense: The trails are blazed but a map is highly recommended as these are long mountain hikes for the most part.

Dog Friendliness
Dogs are not allowed in Watergate Recreation Area that provides access to Van Campens Glen from the north - you will approach from the south.

Traffic
All trails in Worthington State Forest are hiker-only. Van Campens Glen is a popular hiking destination for non-hikers.

Canine Swimming
There is access to the Delaware River along Old Mine Road. Sunfish Pond and Catfish Pond on the Coppermines/Rattlesnake Swamp loop are a water-loving dog's dream.

Trail Time
It would take a busy weekend to cover the 26 miles of trails here.

8
Wharton State Forest

The Park

Wharton State Forest lies at the heart of New Jersey's mysterious Pine Barrens, a tapestry of impenetrable scrub pine, swamps and bogs. Today known for its cranberry and blueberry production, the area's bog ore once supported a booming iron industry which supplied much of the weaponry for the American Revolution. Many of the indecipherable sand roads through the Pine Barrens date to that time.

When the foundries followed the discovery of America's massive upper midwestern iron ranges in the mid-1800s, the area's economy became so depressed that Philadelphia financier Joseph Wharton was able to acquire over 100,000 acres of land here. That land now makes up the state forest - the largest single tract of land in the New Jersey state park system.

Burlington

Phone Number
- (609) 561-0024

Website
- www.state.nj.us/dep/forestry/parks/wharton.htm

Admission Fee
- Parking fee charged weekends in season at Batsto

Directions
- Wharton State Forest has two offices: at Batsto Village on Route 542, eight miles east of Hammonton, and at Atsion Recreation Area on Route 206, eight miles north of Hammonton.

The Walks

The main hiking trail through Wharton State Forest is the *Batona Trail* but for dogs who feel cramped by the rigidness of a narrow 50-mile band there are more than 500 miles of unpaved sand roads in Wharton State Forest.

If that is too much choice, bring your dog to Batsto Village. Thirty-three wooden structures have been restored to this bog iron and glassmaking industrial center which flourished from 1766 to 1867. There is a self-guided one-mile nature walk around the lake at Batsto Village, that includes stops at the Batsto Mansion and an operating gristmill and sawmill.

Trail Sense: Off the Batona Trail you are own your own - do you want to map 500 miles of roads?

The chance to see New Jersey's version of Bigfoot, the legendary winged creature known as the "Jersey Devil." The Jersey Devil is a creature with the head of a horse supported by a four-foot serpentine body with large wings and claws. According to lore, the Devil appeared in the 1700s when an indigent woman named Mrs. Leeds was struggling to feed her 12 children in the darkest recesses of the Pine Barrens. Finding herself once again pregnant she is said to have exclaimed: "I want no more children! Let it be a devil." The devil-child was born horribly deformed, crawled from the womb, up the chimney and into the woods where it was rumored to survive by feeding on small children and livestock, haunting the country-side. When a person saw the Devil, it was an omen of disaster, particularly shipwrecks, to come. Sightings were common through the next two centuries and often breathlessly reported in the local newspapers. Once some local Pineys, as Pine Barrens residents are known, tried to claim a $10,000 reward for capturing the Devil by obtaining a kangaroo, painting stripes across its back and gluing large wings on the animal. But so no documented Jersey Devils have been captured. Perhaps your dog can sniff one out.

Dog Friendliness

Dogs are welcome in the Wharton State Forest.

Traffic

Most of the trails in Wharton State Forest are unimproved dirt roads that hikers share with on-and off-road vehicles. But don't be surprised if you never see anyone.

Canine Swimming

An aquifer inside the Pine Barren's deep sand beds holds 17 trillion gallons of pure glacial water. The shallow aquifer often percolates to the surface in the form of bogs, marshes and swamps. The slow-moving Batsto River is stained the color of tea by cedar sap, adding to the region's mystique. It makes an excellent canine swimming pool - or a wonderful water trail in a canoe.

Trail Time

Many hours - or days - are possible on these trails.

9
Island Beach State Park

The Park

Yes, there is a barrier island in New Jersey where you can stand with your dog and look out at the Atlantic Ocean without being on a boardwalk or a beachhouse deck. Island Beach State Park protects 10 miles of dunesland that have survived virtually untouched as they have always been.

Henry Phipps, compatriot with Andrew Carnegie in U.S. Steel, purchased the island in 1926 with visions of a grand shore resort but the stock market crash halted his assault after erecting a handful of rambling houses.

The Phipps estate sold the property to New Jersey in 1953 and the park opened to the public in 1959.

Ocean

Phone Number
- (732) 793-0506

Website
- http://www.state.nj.us/dep/parksandforests/parks/island.html

Admission Fee
- Yes, higher in summer.

Directions
- From the Garden State Parkway use Exit 82 - Route 37 East/Seaside Heights. Once on the island make a right onto Route 35 South to the park entrance.

The Walks

There are a series of short nature trails (less than one mile) as you drive down the main park road to its end at Barnegat Inlet but once your dog gets that whiff of salt air in her nose, she may not be in any mood to tarry. Get to the beach!

This is one of the few places in New Jersey you can enjoy the Atlantic Ocean with your dog in the summer. Parking is limited, however, and if you don't arrive early enough you will be shut out. In the off-season this is not a problem so don't confine your visits to the novelty of summer at the beach with your dog.

There is some shade for your dog in the dunes and the thickets behind the dunes when it is hot but make sure you bring plenty of fresh water. From the last parking lot to the southern tip of the island is a hike of over one mile on the piles of white sand.

Trail Sense: A park map is available and the nature trails are self-guiding.

Dog Friendliness

Dogs aren't allowed in swimming areas or shorebird nesting areas.

Traffic

With limited parking available if you make it in the park during the summer, you will find stretches of deserted beach. You will be sharing the beach with surf fishermen and off-road vehicles.

Canine Swimming

Ocean swims are why you came.

Trail Time

You can spend most of the day here with your dog.

Active dogs are never at a loss for something to do at Island Beach State Park.

10
Parvin
State Park

The Park

The first landowner of these diverse pinelands was John Estaugh, husband of Elizabeth Haddon, who lived in present-day Haddonfield. Estaugh was granted 2,928 acres on March 31, 1742, by the Proprietors of West Jersey. Development began in 1796 when Lemuel Parvin purchased the property with the intention of operating a sawmill. He created Parvin Lake by constructing an earthen dam across Muddy Run on its journey to the Maurice River.

The State of New Jersey's stewardship began in 1930 with the acquisition of 918 acres of forest and the 108-acre lake. During the Depression of the 1930s the Civilian Conservation Corps established a camp at Parvin, building campgrounds and cabins and carving trails. In 1944, German prisoners of war from Fort Dix were housed in Parvin while working on local farms and food processing plants. The POWS were captured from German Field Marshall Erwin Rommell's marauding Afrika Corps. Many of the facilities built by the Civilian Conservation Corps are still in use in the park today.

Salem

Phone Number
- (609) 358-8616

Website
- www.state.nj.us/dep/forestry/parks/parvin.htm

Admission Fee
- None

Directions
- Parvin State Park is six miles west of Vineland on Route 540, just east of the intersection with Route 553.

The Walks

A variety of loops and linear trails slice across Parvin State Park's 1,135 acres, about evenly divided between a recreational area and a natural area. The canine hiking is easier in the recreational area with its wide, packed-sand trails; paths narrow in the oak-pine forests, cedar swamps and laurel thickets of the natural area. These scenic woodlands on the fringe of the Pine Barrens are home to 40 known types of trees and 61 different woody shrubs as southern United States ecosystems collide with northern species at the southern tip of their natural range. All the hiking with your dog is on nine named trails, totalling more than 15 miles, and is easy-going for any dog.

> _Bonus_
> For the dog who favors entering the water with a
> well-executed belly flop there are boat docks available,
> including a wide wooden pier stretching 25 yards into
> Lake Parvin for Dock Diving pracitice.

Trail Sense: Only trailheads on the major trails are marked and trail blazes disappear in the natural area. Don't let go of the park map on long hikes.

Dog Friendliness
All trails are open to dogs but they are not permitted in the campgrounds and cabins and in the Parvin Grove beach area.

Traffic
This is not a heavily used park and away from the campgrounds and picnic groves isolation can be realized. Only a few trails are hiker-only, however.

Canine Swimming
There is excellent doggie paddling in the attractive Parvin Lake and there is abundant access to the water in smaller Thundergast Lake. Although access is limited, the swimming is also good in the deceptively-named Muddy Run.

Trail Time
Several hours of canine hiking are on the menu here.

II
Hacklebarney
State Park

The Park

In the 1800s settlers mined this area for veins of iron ore exposed by the retreating glaciers. It is believed by some that the colorful name for the park came from workmen in a mine who heckled a petulant foreman named Barney Tracey. "Heckle Barney eventually morphed into Hacklebarney.

Others believe the name has Lenni-Lenape Indian origins based on the word for ground, "Haki." Park staff apparently buy into this theory since there is a *Haki Trail* and no Tracey Trail.

Adolph E. Borie (who also has no trail) donated the first 32 acres of land in 1924 as a memorial to his mother and niece, a Titanic survivor. The Civilian Conservation Corps helped develop the park during the 1930s and today it consists of nearly 1000 acres of Black River glacial valley.

Morris

Phone Number
- (609) 861-2404

Website
- http://www.state.nj.us/dep/parksandforests/parks/hackle.html

Admission Fee
- None

Directions
- From the town of Chester Follow Route 24/513 west for one mile to State Park Road for two miles. Turn right onto Hacklebarney Road and travel 1/2 mile. The entrance is on the left. From Pottersville, take Pottersville Road (partially paved) right of the Black River and turn left on Hacklebarney.

The Walks

There are some five miles of sporty canine hiking in Hacklebarney State Park to enjoy with your dog. Most of the park can be experienced on the red-blazed *Main Trail* that sweeps down the ravine to the Black River and comes back up the opposite side. The trail drops about 200 feet in elevation to the water and this is negotiated on wide, graded gravelly footpaths.

Along the rollicking Black River the trail is narrow and rocky with a different angle of footfall on every step. Your dog can take a misstep here as easily as you can so take care. The ravine along the water is dominated by thick Eastern hemlock trees that keep this walk cool for your dog even in the summer heat.

Trail Sense: The trails are color-coded and well-marked; a trail map is available.

Dog Friendliness
Dogs are allowed on the Hacklebarney State Park trails.

Traffic
Foot traffic only - no bikes and no horses in the park.

Canine Swimming
The rushing Black River waters slow into pools a few times to provide a refreshing doggie dip. Coincidentally when this happens there is usually a small dirt beach for easy access.

Trail Time
Expect to spend between one and two hours on these trails.

The hydrospectacular Black River is a natural spa for dogs.

12

Jenny Jump
State Forest

The Park

Mile-thick glaciers did the carving of ridges and valleys in this forest and littered giant boulders about for decoration. There are several legends surrounding the name "Jenny Jump."

The most dramatic has little Jenny out picking berries with her father when they were surprised by hostile Indians. Preferring the fate of a leap off an exposed cliff to capture by Indians for his daughter, the father yelled for Jenny to jump. And so she did, to her death.

Kinder, gentler versions have Jenny and her father transporting a wagon of homemade beer and Jenny jumping off the kegs and fleeing to safety or Jenny leaping from a precipice to avoid an unwanted suitor and being rescued at the base of the cliff by her true love.

Warren

Phone Number
- (908) 459-4366

Website
- http://www.state.nj.us/dep/parksandforests/parks/jenny-jump.html

Admission Fee
- None

Directions
- Take I-80 to Exit 12 to Hope. Turn onto Route 519 north at blinking light. At the third right, turn onto Shiloh Road. After aproximately one mile turn right onto State Park Road.

The Walks

The main canine hiking in Jenny Jump State Forest is along the *Summit Trail* that rambles up and down along a 1,090-foot high ridge. The trailhead is almost at that elevation so the climb will scarcely get your dog panting. Although you will be picking your way among huge boulders on the ridge your dog will find the footing to be paw-friendly dirt.

Several trails intersect the ridge and many dog walkers will want to use the *Orchard Trail* to complete a loop hike through a picnic area built by Civilian Conservation Corps workers in the 1930s. Depending on how long you dally at panoramic viewpoints of the Jersey Highlands and the Delaware Water Gap this will make a compact exploration of the forest of little more than an hour.

Adventurous canine hikers can drop off the ridge on the *Ghost Lake Trail* that leads to a man-made lake fed by an artesian well. This lake is only about ten feet deep and becomes choked with vegetation, including yellow-blooming water lilies in the summer. This trail doesn't loop so you will have to climb about 400 feet back up the mountain unless you have employed a car shuttle linked to the Ghost Lake parking lot.

Trail Sense: The trails are well-blazed and a map is available to keep you oriented on the ridge.

Dog Friendliness
Dogs are allowed throughout the forest but cannot stay in the campground.

Traffic
Some of the trails permit bikes but there is mostly solitude in the Jenny Jump State Forest.

Canine Swimming
Ghost Lake provides a venue for canine aquatics.

Trail Time
A half-day's canine hiking will completely cover these trails.

The shallow Ghost Lake fills with water lillies int he summer.

43

13

Wawayanda State Park

The Park

When the New Jersey Zinc Company was here they saw the miles of trees as fuel for timbering their mines. When Fred Ferber, an Austrian immigrant who helped pioneer the ballpoint pen, bought 6,800 acres of timberland from New Jersey Zinc he saw wilderness that needed to be preserved. Not as a public park. Ferber chased hunters from the land and railed against such facilities as toilets and campgrounds in the woods.

When Ferber ran into financial reversals he was forced to sell portions of his land to the state over the years that would become exactly what he hated - Wawayanda State Park, a recreational mecca for boaters, fishermen, campers, picnicers, swimmers, hunters and, yes, hikers.

Sussex/Passaic

Phone Number
- (973) 853-4462

Website
- www.state.nj.us/dep/parksand-forests/parks/wawayanda.html

Admission Fee
- Charged in the summer in the recreation areas

Directions
- Take Route 23 north to Union Valley Road and go about six miles to stop sign. From the stop sign, go to second traffic light. Turn left, travel to fork in road (about 2 miles) and go left about 1/2 mile to Warwick Turnpike. Turn left. The park entrance is four miles on the left.

The Walks

Spread across 16,679 acres are more than 40 miles of trails, many on old logging roads that make for easy, although often active, canine hiking. There are three major destinations in the park:

Wawayanda Hemlock Ravine Natural Area. There is only one trail through this hemlock/hardwoods preserve, a stretch o the *Appalachian Trail* so you will need to retrace your steps on any explorations here. The steep hemlock ravine features 300-foot increases in elevation change.

Wawayanda Swamp Natural Area. This is the dominant central section of the park with Laurel Pond, a small glacial lake, a quick destination on an old gravel road. Other trails delve deeper into this rare inland Atlantic white cedar

44

swamp. This is also a good place for your dog to spot a beaver at work.

Bearfort Mountain Natural Area. The most famous hike at Wawayanda State Park, the four-mile loop to Terrace Pond, is found here. The hike is a pleasant ramble through mixed forests at the beginning and end but the payoff at the boulder-ringed lake is one of the most challenging your dog can take in New Jersey. From

It is quite a canine hike to reach this payoff on the rocky shores of Terrace Pond.

the parking lot located on Clinton Road, it is suggested to take your dog on the Yellow-White-Blue route rather than starting in the blue-blazed direction (to the left). This is because the considerable rock hopping required is easier going down than climbing up on the *Blue Trail*. Take it slow any way you go because your dog will do a great deal of jumping around Terrace Pond.

Trail Sense: There is a park map that shows the location of the trails but a trail map would be more valuable. Pay attention as some of the blazes are maddeningly similar (is that the yellow trail or the yellow dot trail...)

Dog Friendliness
Dogs are permitted on the trails but not in the campgrounds or swimming areas.
Traffic
Many of the road-type trails are frequented by mountain bikes and horses; in the summer you may want to sample some of lesser-known trails.
Canine Swimming
There are plenty of lakes here to get your dog a good swim.
Trail Time
A full day of canine hiking if your dog wants it.

14
Higbee Beach WMA

The Park

Higbee Beach, the last remaining dune forest along the Delaware Bay, was acquired by the State of New Jersey in 1978, thwarting plans to build a campground here. The Higbee Beach Wildlife Management Area today is jointly administered by the state and the U.S. Army Corps of Engineers.

For years Higbee Beach was known as the area's "nude beach" but now your dog is the only visitor legally allowed to hit the beach without a swim suit.

The Walks

How can you tell in a hurry if your dog will be welcome in a park? When

Cape May

Phone Number
- (609) 628-2103

Website
- http://www.njfishandwildlife.com/ensp/higbee.htm

Admission Fee
- None

Directions
- From Route 9 south, turn onto Route 626. Cross the bridge and turn right onto New England Road (Route 641). The road deadends at Higbee Beach into a wildly rutted dirt parking lot.

you see the rusting carcass of an old car - possibly a Corvair - along the trail you can probably assume this is a place you'll be allowed to hike with your dog.

You can't beat the canine hiking at Higbee Beach for diversity. From the parking lot at land's end on the Cape May Peninsula you have your choice of open fields, woodlands or dune forest. Of course, your dog will want to sample all three.

The sandhills are not covered with windswept grasses as is seen along most of the Jersey shore but with resilient red cedars and holly trees. There is about a mile of trails meandering through this dunesland. Your dog is welcome on the soft sand paths and on the wide Delaware Bay beaches they lead to. While these trails aren't long the sand is deep and expect your dog to tire much quicker than on a dirt trail.

To stretch those leg muscles there are several miles of more trails behind the dunes in the woods and fields of the wildlife management area that reaches all the way to the Cape May Canal.

Trail Sense: There are color-coded signposts in the dunes but with no map available there is no way to make much sense of them for the first-time visitor. You won't need a bloodhound to get back to your car, however.

Your dog doesn't get many chances to romp on sand dunes in New Jersey like at Higbee Beach.

Dog Friendliness
Dogs can hike the trails and enjoy the beaches at Higbee Beach Wildlife Management Area.

Traffic
With more than a mile of beach here you can most always claim a stretch for yourself after dodging birders you may meet on the trail.

Canine Swimming
It doesn't get any better for dogs than on the beach at the Delaware Bay.

Trail Time
A couple hours is possible but your dog won't be in any hurry to leave Higbee Beach.

15

Morristown National Historic Park

The Park

Morristown, a village of 250, was a center of iron supply for the American Revolution and even though it lay only 30 miles west of the main British force in New York it was protected by a series of parallel mountain ranges. It was the twin luxuries of a defensible position and close proximity to the enemy that twice brought General George Washington to camp his main army here, first in 1777 and again in 1779-1780.

After the Battle of Princeton in January 3, 1777 a worn-down Washington's Colonial army swarmed the tiny town seeking shelter in the few public buildings, private homes, barns and stables then in existence. Steadily Washington rebuilt his flagging troops, overcoming desertion and insipient food shortages. His greatest foe, however, was disease. An outbreak of smallpox threatened to decimate the small army and Washington ordered the little known and, to many, horrifying procedure of innoculation. Some indeed died but most of his troops did not contract the deadly pox.

The park was created in 1933 as America's first national historic park.

Morris

Phone Number
- (973) 543-4030

Website
- http://www.nps.gov/morr/

Admission Fee
- Yes; daily or annual pass.

Directions
- The park is located along I-287. Traveling south on I-287, use Exit 36; traveling north on 287, exit at 36A. Look for the signs for Jockey Hollow.

The Walks

Canine hiking at Morristown National Historic Park is found at the Jockey Hollow Encampment Area. When here, nothing could have prepared the Continental Army for the worst winter of the 18th century. Twenty-eight blizzards pounded the slopes and whipped through the wooden huts that were cut from 600 acres of hardwood forests here.

The forest has grown back and is open and airy with long views through the trees from the trail. Four main trails circle the Jockey Hollow Encampment.

The 6.5-mile *Grand Loop Trail*, blazed in white, circles the park but doesn't visit any historical attractions without a detour. It is also the only trail that cannot be accessed from the centrally located Trail Center.

The *Aqueduct Loop Trail* and the stacked loop *Primrose Brook Trail* are two of the prettiest rambles in the park as they trace some of the many gurgling streams that once served the Colonial Army.

The long-distance *Patriot's Path* traces its lineage back to 1966 and links Jockey Hollow to the New Jersey Encampment Area and neighboring parks and contributes mightily to the total of 27 well-groomed miles of Morristown trails.

Trail Sense: All the junctions on these first-rate trails feature directional signs and park maps.

Dog Friendliness
Dogs are welcome on these national park trails.
Traffic
Maybe folks are scared off by the word "historical" but this is a delightfully under-utilized trail system, especially during the week.
Canine Swimming
A few streams pool lazily into small ponds at times but this is not the place to bring your dog for a swim.
Trail Time
A half-day and more is possible.

Huts like this one were forced to house 15 Revolutionary soldiers.

The trails at Morristown Historical Park are well-signed.

16

Huber Woods Park

The Park

Joseph Maria Huber sailed for New York City from his native Bavaria in 1883 as a sales agent for his family's ink-pigment business. Once in America it didn't take him long to see opportunities for a hard-working ink supplier. Before the decade was out Huber was so successful that he bought out the American stake of the business from his German relatives—and launched J.M. Huber Corporation. Four generations later the multinational supplier of engineered materials is one of the largest family-owned companies in the United States.

Huber Woods Park is the result of a 118-acre gift of land from the Huber family in 1974. Ongoing acquisition in the same spirit of land preservation has doubled the size of the present-day park.

Monmouth

Phone Number
- (732) 872-2670

Website
- www.monmouthcountyparks.com/parks/huber.asp

Admission Fee
- None

Directions
- The park is east of the Garden State Parkway. Take State Highway 35 to Navesink River Road. Travel east for 2.8 miles and turn left onto Brown's Dock Road (unimproved). The park entrance is on the right at the top of the hill.

The Walks

It is hard to imagine a more pleasant place to hike with your dog in New Jersey than at Huber Woods. The six-mile trail system offers any length of outing from a half-hour to a half-day. You can stay completely within an airy, mixed hardwood forest or cross Brown's Dock Road to include open fields on the *Meadow Ramble Trail*. In spring on the short *Nature Loop*, azaelas and later mountain laurel bursts into bloom. The trails roll up and down hills but never in a way that will leave your dog panting.

Once you have explored the hollows and valleys of the woodlands cross to the other side of the parking lot and try the *Farm Path*, an equestrian trail

that passes through fields managed to maintain the pastoral feel of the Huber
farm.

Trail Sense: There is a trailmap available and the trails are marked and
signed. You will encounter a rogue trail or two that isn't on the map.

Dog Friendliness
Dogs are permitted on the park's trails.
Traffic
All the longer trails have been designed for equestrian and all-terrain bicycle
use. If you want to share the trail with walkers only, start with the *Fox Hollow*
loop.
Canine Swimming
None.
Trail Time
Up to several hours is possible.

17
Palisades
Interstate Park

The Park

If millions of Americans didn't already live in the area by the time we got around to setting aside land for parks it is not hard to imagine the 500-foot sheer cliffs of the Palisades being a national park right now. The cliffs formed 200 million years ago when molten volcanic material cooled and solidified before reaching the surface. Subsequent water erosion of the softer sandstone substrate left behind the columnar structure of harder rock that exists today.

The hard stone, known locally as traprock, was enthusiastically quarried for buildings and roads in the New York area until 1900 when governors

Bergen

Phone Number
- (201) 768-1360

Website
- www.njpalisades.org

Admission Fee
- None

Directions
- From I-95 take the exit for Fort Lee / Palisades Interstate Parkway (Exit 72, after the last toll on the New Jersey Turnpike). Turn left at the light at the top of the ramp. Go through several lights in succession, then the entrance to the northbound PIP is on right.

Theodore Roosevelt of New York and Foster Voorhees of New Jersey created the Palisades Interstate Park Commission to save this dramatic Hudson River landscape.

Today's park meanders about 12 miles along the river - never more than a half-a-mile wide - and preserves 2,500 acres of wild Hudson River shorefront and uplands, including some of the most impressive sections of the Palisades.

The Walks

Two long-distance trails - the aqua-blazed *Long Path* atop the Palisades and the white-blazed *Shore Path* along the river - traverse the length of the park. Occasional, and very steep, connectors (sometimes using steps) connect the two that enable canine hiking loops. Every now and then the Long Path touches on the edge of the impressive cliffs and there are spots an overly-curious dog could squeeze under the fence, so be careful. On top of the Palisades the going is mostly easy but does roll through varied woodlands that will distract you from the spectacular views at times. You can also find extra trail time for your dog on cross-country ski paths if you don't want to walk for miles along the cliffs.

The iconic hike at Palisades is "The Giant Stairs" located beneath State Line Lookout. The Giant Stairs are massive boulders that have piled up at the foot of the cliffs from thousands of rock slides over millions of years. You need to scramble for over a mile to complete a 3.5-mile loop at the north end of the park. Unless your dog is light enough to lift DO NOT attempt this with your dog. Is it possible? Yes. Is it fun. NO. In addition to being a difficult traverse for dogs there are hundreds of hiding places in the rocks for venomous copperhead snakes and dogs have been bitten at Palisades Interstate Park.

Swimming in the Hudson River beneath the Palisades is a relief for dogs after the Giant Stairs.

Trail Sense: The trails are well-marked and signed and there are detailed trail maps available, dividing the park into three sections.

Dog Friendliness
Dogs are permitted on the trails.

Traffic
Most people come for the views or to relax atop the Palisades. Canine hikers will find less activity down on the Shore Path.

Canine Swimming
There are small beaches - some sand and some pebbly - that allow great access into the Hudson River for doggie aquatics.

Trail Time
Many, many hours if so desired.

18
Cattus Island County Park

The Park

Back in 1690 the Board of Proprietors for the Province of East Jersey carved up the property along these shores. Ever since, Cattus Island has remained a single parcel of land.

During the Revolutionary War, patriots used the peninsula to off-load cargo from captured British frigates. In quieter times farmers harvested salt hay from the marshes.

At the turn of the 20th century, John V.A. Cattus, a New York importer, purchased the property to use as a hunting and boating retreat. In 1914, he became the charter Commodore of the Barnegat Bay Racing Association.

Private owners bought Cattus Island in 1961 but before it could be developed the New Jersey Wetlands Act of 1970 saved it for open space. The county began construction of the trail system in 1977.

Ocean

Phone Number
- (877) 921-0074

Website
- http://www.co.ocean.nj.us/parks/cattus.html

Admission Fee
- None

Directions
- Cattus Island is in Toms River. From the Garden State Parkway use Exit 82 - Route 37 East/Seaside Heights. Take the jughandle to Fischer Boulevard and head north. Turn right at the fourth light onto Cattus Island Boulevard. The parking lot is on the left.

The Walks

A paved and unpaved road runs for one mile down the spine of the 500-acre Cattus Island peninsula. Two main trails loop across the road and a smaller loop radiates off it near the end for a total of five miles of walking paths. Come here for relaxed canine hiking on level paths through the maritime forests and salt marshes.

The *Island Loop* snakes around for a little more than two miles under a wooded canopy. Stop along the way at a bird blind to check on activity at one of several osprey poles in the marshes. At the parking lot is the 1.7-mile *Maritime Forest Loop* that is a landlocked exploration for your dog. The *Hidden Beach*

Loop at the end of Cattus Island uses a boardwalk to cross onto a small island of forest. The Boy Scouts have sculpted a paw-friendly trail of wood shavings and soft dirt that makes an ideal destination for a canine hike.

Trail Sense: A trail map is available at the Cooper Environmental Center and mapboards can be consulted if the center is closed. The color-coded loop trails are well-marked but it helps to know where to look for the trailheads.

Dog Friendliness
Dogs are allowed throughout the park.

Traffic
This is primarily a park for hikers; bikes are restricted to the roadways. Get off the main road to avoid the regular park users.

Canine Swimming
Cattus Island is one of the best places in New Jersey to take your dog for a swim. The Island Loop touches briefly on the frisky waves of Mosquito Cove from a small sand beach and a longer stretch of sand on the open waters of the Silver Bay at the end of the unpaved road will excite any dog. If your dog prefers a more peaceful body of water try the namesake patch of sand on the Barnegat Bay from the Hidden Beach Loop.

Trail Time
Several hours of canine hiking will only leave you wanting more trail time at Cattus Island.

19
Sourland Mountain Preserve

The Park

Sourland Mountain is at the northeast point of a ridge of sedimentary and igneous rock that was deposited between 150 and 180 million years ago and stretches to the Delaware River. It is hard to believe walking the thickly wooded mountainside but this was once a treeless farm.

After picking your way through the boulders strewn across the Preserve it is easy to imagine that the name "Sourland" comes from the farmers who abandoned growing crops in favor of grazing cows but it actually is believed to derive from the term "sorrel-land" to describe the reddish-brown colored soils.

Somerset

Phone Number
- None

Website
- http://www.mercercounty.org/parks/parks.htm

Admission Fee
- None

Directions
- From Route 206 (South Broad Street), turn onto West Park Avenue. Make a left turn onto Wescott Avenue. After passing under high tension wires, make an immediate right turn onto the lane that leads to the park.

The Walks

Sourland Mountain features three blazed trails, the star being the 5-mile *Ridge Trail*. The trail pushes uphill away from the parking lot - not too strenuously but expect to see your dog start panting - until it reaches a picturesque cluster of boulders. The elevation gain is about 300 feet. After this the trail flattens out and is a comfortable walk with your dog in airy woodsland on a wide path.

The Ridge Trail can be aborted with a walk down a cut-away for a pipeline. This is the only open-air hiking at Sourland Mountain and you can enjoy the views on the way down. On a clear day it is possible to see New York City.

If the 300-foot climb seems more hike than your dog is looking for, you can still enjoy Sourland Mountain. The *Maple Flats* and *Pondside* trails break off from the Ridge Trail before heading up the mountain. The two form a stacked-loop trail that together totals less than two miles.

Trail Sense: The trails are enthusiastically blazed with geometric-shaped disks that are helpful in the boulder fields. There is also an excellent topographic map to carry along and numbered interesection posts with arrows indicating the direction of the trail. The only wayfinding aid they have missed is a guide dog.

Dog Friendliness
Dogs are welcome to explore Sourland Mountain.

Traffic
This is a popular spot for birders as the lower slopes are wide open; the Ridge Trail gets considerably less use.

Canine Swimming
Aide from the pond there is no swimming here; the mountain streams are barely deep enough for wading.

Trail Time
Several hours.

Your dog will look forward to scaling the boulder field atop Sourland Mountain.

20
Ramapo Valley County Reservation

The Park

Ramapo translates roughly to "round ponds." There are hydro-delights aplenty in this Bergen County park - lakes and waterfalls - as well as great views across Bergen County to New York City.

These forested mountains were a strategic route drung the Revolution and later a favorite camping spot for the Boy Scouts before the county began acquiring the land for the 2,000-acre park.

Bergen

Phone Number
- None

Website
- None

Admission Fee
- None

Directions
- From I-287 take Exit 66 onto Route 17 South and then Route 202 South. Drive about two miles and turn right into the parking area (about .5 of a mile south of Ramapo College).

The Walks

There are at least 15 miles of marked trails across Ramapo Mountain, doled out in trail segments in the system. The choice of loops - or even a long car shuttle - is yours. One of the more popular - if ambitious - destinations is Bear Swamp Lake where you can see the scars of a modern day battle. Developers were the loser in this war and you can poke around chimneys and foundations and abandoned patios as remnants of the defeat.

If some of the popular trails seem too popular there are many options on these wide woods roads and footpaths created under many a Boy Scout hoe. The Ramapos only rise to about 1,200 feet and your dog won't find much in the way of strenuous trotting here so you may want to spend extra time on these trails, maybe even exploring neighboring parks like Ramapo State Forest.

Trail Sense: The park trails are reliably blazed and a keyed trail map is a must for lengthy explorations.

Dog Friendliness
   Dogs are allowed on these trails.
Traffic
   Bikes and horses and plenty of fellow dogs.
Canine Swimming
   Absolutely - plan a route to visit at least one lake.
Trail Time
   Several hours.

"He is very imprudent, a dog is. He never makes it his business to inquire whether you are in the right or in the wrong, never bothers as to whether you are going up or down upon life's ladder, never asks whether you are rich or poor, silly or wise, sinner or saint."

-Jerome K. Jerome

21

Mountain Lakes Preserve

The Park

This land was part of the original land grant to William Penn and was an active farm for more than 100 years.

In the 1880s the Margerum family constructed a system of earthen and concrete dams to create the two namesake lakes and began selling ice. Look closely and you can see foundations of large barns used for ice storage on the western slopes of the lakes. The bustling ice business continued until 1930.

The original park was created in 1987 when the Friends of Open Space helped purchase a 70-acre private estate. Additional parcels of land were welded onto Mountain Lakes to create Princeton's "Central Park." The eastern section includes part of the Tusculum estate, home of John Witherspoon, who added his name to the Declaration of Independence.

Mercer

Phone Number
- (609) 924-8720

Website
- http://www.princetontwp.org/mtnlakes.html

Admission Fee
- None

Directions
- Take Route 206 North out of Princeton. Look for the sign for Mountain Avenue and exit into the jughandle. Cross over 206 and the parking lot is immediately on the right.

The Walks

Attacking the trail system at Mountain Lakes Nature Preserve requires a two-stage plan. First, study one of the two detailed mapboards in the parking lot. Then exit the parking lot to the left and make your way to the paved driveway that leads to the Mountain Lakes House. You will need to hike your dog a ways up this driveway to the Trail Kiosk where a trail map can be had. Now you can start.

There are seven miles of rambles with your dog here spread across three distinct segments of property, each with its own personality. The blue-blazed *James Sayen Trail* system circumnavigates the mountain lakes on dirt and mown grass trails that are easy-going for any dog. In the northern end of the park, reached with some mild climbing into the John Witherspoon Woods, drops into an old-growth forest that has sprung up in a boulder field created by a volcanic intrusion that formed Princeton Ridge. Your dog will find the going a bit more challenging through this section.

Returning to the parking lot through Community Park North you descend into a nicely-spaced scented pine grove before crossing a grass-covered sewer line into a garden area to finish your canine hike.

Trail Sense: The trails are blazed with metallic disks - but the colored markers don't indicate any particular route. Instead they indicate which of the three sections of the park you are in.

Dog Friendliness
Dogs are allowed on all these trails.
Traffic
This is a popular park for dog walkers.
Canine Swimming
There is easy access for dogs into the mountain lakes for playful canine aquatics.
Trail Time
You can spend up to half a day hiking with your dog at Mountain Lakes.

22
Mahlon Dickerson Reservation

The Park

This park is the largest facility in the Morris County Park System, and with more than 3,000 acres can easily be mistaken for a rustic state park. It is named for one of the Garden State's most accomplished citizens, Mahlon Dickerson, born in Hanover Township in 1770.

Dickerson graduated from Princeton in 1793, having mastered several foreign languages and was soon admitted to the New Jersey Bar. He owned and operated iron mines and was widely known for his work in botany.

Dickerson was appointed to the New Jersey Supreme Court in 1813 and before his political career was over he had served as governor and United States Senator.

Morris

Phone Number
- (973) 326-7631

Website
- www.morrisparks.net/parks/mahlonmain.htm

Admission Fee
- None

Directions
- From I-80 exit onto Route 15 North. Proceed for 5 miles to the Weldon Road Exit and travel approximately 4 miles east. Signed parking lots can be found on both sides of the road.

The Walks

This is a canine hiker's trail system. Your dog can stretch his legs on the wide old logging roads that make up most of the 20 miles of trails. Save for Headley Overlook (beware of false overlooks if you approach from the south!) and its east-facing views there are no great destinations at Mahlon Dickerson, just miles of rambling under a solid canopy of mixed forest. On the way you'll pass through interesting rock formations, dank hemlock groves and thick stands of laurel.

Although the average elevation in the park is over 1,200 feet the ups and downs are never grueling. The high point tops out at 1,388 feet along the *Pine Swamp Trail* but there are no views here. Several stream crossings add flavor to your dog's expedition in Mahlon Dickerson. If you start your explorations at Saffin Pond she will have an ideal pool to cool off in after the hike.

Trail Sense: The trails are well-blazed and signed and an excellent trail map is available - but not in every parking lot. Stop at the Saffin Visitor Center (the first parking lot approaching from the south) at Saffin Rock-Rill to pick one up.

Dog Friendliness
Dogs are allowed on all the trails at Mahlon Dickerson Reservation.
Traffic
Some trails support horse traffic and some support bike travel but this is a big place. The teal-marked *Highlands Trail* is a good choice for foot traffic-only canine hiking.
Canine Swimming
Saffin Pond is centralized and convenient for a doggie dip but out on the trails there is only splashing in streams.
Trail Time
You can spend all day hiking with your dog at Mahlon Dickerson.

23

Ringwood State Park

The Park

The Ringwood Company put a dam across the Ringwood River and used the water power to operate blast furnaces and forges. For the next 200 years some of America's most famous ironmasters toiled here.

The ironworks hit its stride when Scotsman Robert Erskine was hired in 1771. Under his stewardship Ringwood supplied a steady stream of weapons for the American Revolution. Upon meeting George Washington the general was so impressed with Erskine he made him Surveyor General for the Colonial Army. The ironmaster made some 275 detailed maps that Washington relied on in his maneuvers in the Northeast. Erskine however caught pneumonia and died on a mapping expedition in 1780.

In the mid-1800s Ringwood came under control of Abram S. Hewitt, the pre-eminent American ironmaster. His descendents deeded the Ringwood Manor House and property to the State of New Jersey for a park in 1936.

Passaic

Phone Number
- (973) 962-7031

Website
- nj.gov/dep/parksandforests/
parks/ringwood.html

Admission Fee
- None if you are not using the Shepherd Lake Recreation Area or visiting the manor houses.

Directions
- From I-287 take Exit 55 and head north on Greenwood Lake Road (Route 511) heading north. Make a right at Sloatsburg Road (it is not marked) to the park. If you go completley past Wanaque Reservoir, you've gone too far.

The Walks

The Ringwood trail system ties into the Ramapo Mountain State Forest system to the west and into Bergen County parkland to the east. Volunteers have carved so many trails into the New Jersey highlands your dog could start out sampling them as a puppy and return a senior dog before hiking them all. Some trails serve to connect the two sections of the park, Ringwood and Skylands.

Expect a diverse woodland that has regenerated around Ringwood, including fine cedars and shady hemlocks. The area is peppered with glacial erratics but rock scrambling is not a big factor for your dog here - extensive use is made of the old road system from the ironworks.

Some of the more popular canine hikes explore the areas around the manor houses while those in search of rocky vistas can try the yellow-blazed *Cooper Union Trail* that explores Governor Mountain. The original trail was laid out by members of the Cooper Union Hiking club from the prestigious Manhattan college founded by one of New Jersey's largest landowners, Peter Cooper.

Trail Sense: Trails maps are available and are essential for deeper explorations of this vast region.

Dog Friendliness
Dogs are permitted in the non-recreation areas of the park.
Traffic
The popular Ringwood trails have been well-trod but away from the manor houses there is plenty of room to escape the crowds. The undeveloped roads in the park attract equestrians, mountain bikers and, in the winter, skiers and snowmobilers.
Canine Swimming
There are many ponds in these mountains.
Trail Time
As much as your dog wants.

*"Dog. A kind of additional or subsidiary Deity
designed to catch the overflow and surplus
of the world's worship."*
-Ambrose Bierce

24

Six Mile Run Reservoir Site

The Park

In 1970 the State of New Jersey acquired more than 3,000 acres with an eye towards creating a reservoir site. That day never came and in 1993 alternative water sources were discovered and the Division of Parks and Forestry became the new stewards of the land.

The park is administered as a part of the Delaware and Raritan Canal State Park. Much of the land is leased to the public but there is plenty of hiking space left to entice visitors to make the journey to this out-of-the-way natural area.

The Walks

Six Mile Run refers to the stream

Somerset

Phone Number
- (609) 924-5705

Website
- http://www.dandrcanal.com/interest.html

Admission Fee
- None

Directions
- The park is west of New Brunswick. From Route 514 West take a left onto Route 533. Make a left on Blackwell Mills Road in about 2.5 miles. Cross the canal and make a right on Canal Road; the parking lot is on the left.

that feeds into the Raritan River but it could almost apply to the 6.2 miles of trail here. There are three color-coded trails to try with your dog. You will most likely push away on the *Blue Trail* behind the parking lot, longest of the trio. Your dog starts in open fields before eventually ducking into the woods.

A good choice for the canine hiker is to come back on the *Yellow Trail* that traces the Six Mile Run before finishing at the old park office after a short field walk. Your dog will enjoy the soft dirt in the floodplain and the frequent access to the shallow water but you may be slogging through some muck when it's wet.

The 1.5-mile *Red Trail* serves up what could be called rugged fare at Six Mile Reservoir Site. There are stream crossings and an occasional scamper up a slope through open fields and groves of cedar trees. The Red Trail also connects with the Blue Trail to form a 5.3-mile loop. The hike from the parking lot to the trailhead for the Red Trail covers only 200 yards but it is on a narrow, semi-busy roadway along the canal.

For extended canine hiking you can cross the road and take off on a jaunt down the Delaware and Raritan Canal towpath. This is a relaxed rural stretch of the popular canal trail that runs from New Brunswick to Bordentown.

Trail Sense: The park office has relocated and there may not be any trail maps in the box. The trails are reliably marked, however, and you should have no trouble making your way back to the parking lot.

Dog Friendliness

Dogs are welcome on the Six Mile Run trails.

Traffic

These trails are lightly visited; bikes and horses on part of the Blue Trail.

Canine Swimming

Small dogs might find some dog paddling in the Six Mile Run but it's mostly for splashing or a great spot to lie in on a hot summer day.

Trail Time

A couple hours or more is possible.

25
High Point State Park

The Park

Colonel Anthony Kuser, founding member of the New Jersey Audubon Society and director of more than 50 corporations, and his wife Susie Dryden, daughter of Senator John Fairfield Dryden, founder of the Prudential Life Insurance Company, made the largest land donation in the history of New Jersey when they deeded 11,000 acres for High Point State Park in 1923.

The Kusers had purchased the High Point Inn in 1910 and transformed it into a transcendent wildlfe sanctuary. To help complete the transition from country estate to public park the Olmsted Brothers, sons of Central Park creator Fredeick Law Olmsted, were retained to landscape the mountaintop.

Sussex

Phone Number
- (973) 875-4800

Website
- http://www.state.nj.us/dep/
parksandforests/parks/high-
point.html

Admission Fee
- None

Directions
- In the far northwest corner of the state travel on Route 23 for seven miles north of the town of Sussex to the park entrance.

The Walks

The park maintains an 11-trail system around the 1,803-foot summit at the top of New Jersey. You can choose to hike with your dog on wide, manicured paths or take off on rock-strewn mountain trails. Most visitors will want to be certain to sample two choice items on the canine hiking menu at High Point State Park.

Leaving from the far end of the parking lot at the High Point Monument, the trail tops the ridge in light woods with abundant views east and west. The narrow path is rocky as it rolls along but completely manageable for any dog.

Below the ridge you will find the 1,500-acre Dryden Kuser Natural Area, created in 1965 and site of some of the most pleasant canine hiking in the state. The Atlantic white cedars here are normally found only in the Pine Barrens of south Jersey. This cedar swamp is at the highest elevation of any of its kind in the world. The swamp trail is level and wide and shouldn't be missed by any dog who visits the top of New Jersey. There is also extended canine hiking available on the *Appalachian Trail* that crosses through the park.

Trail Sense: The park is well spread out and a map is available to get you to various hiking sections.

Dog Friendliness
Dogs are allowed to stand on the highest patch of ground in New Jersey.

Traffic
The further you push off the ridge the less folks you will encounter on the trail.

Canine Swimming
Hiking trails around the High Point Monument will not lead to extended swimming for your dog although there are ponds in the park.

Trail Time
The canine hiking loop for the cedar swamp and the monument will take several hours; a full day can be spent exploring all the trails.

26
Estell
Manor Park

The Park

The first deed granting land to the Estell family in this area appeared in 1677. During Colonial times the Estells were among the largest landowners in Atlantic County. In 1825 a glassworks was established by the Estells using the bottomless supplies of Jersey sand to best advantage.

During World War I industry came to the Great Egg Harbor River in a big way. The Bethlehem Loading Company munitions plant churned out more than 50,000 large caliber shells in little more than one year before shutting down in 1919. A complete town of 3,000 people sprung up to support the bustling plant.

For nearly a century the forest has been reclaiming the area and today the 1,700-acre Estell Manor Park is the most popular in the Atlantic County Park System.

Atlantic

Phone Number
- (609) 645-5960

Website
- http://www.aclink.org/PARKS/mainpages/estell.asp

Admission Fee
- None

Directions
- The park is located on Route 50, 3.5 miles south of Mays Landing.

The Walks

There is plenty of to do in this busy park and canine hikers will do best to turn north and leave the ballfields and exercise trail and fishing docks to others. The trail system in the North End is built largely upon many of the 24 miles of abandoned railway built by the Bethlehem Loading Company. These leveled paths are soft and wide and perfect for any dog. Almost all of your canine hiking here will be under the canopy of a shaded, mature forest.

Estell Manor maintains about 13 miles of trail, including almost two miles of elevated boardwalk across a cedar swamp. Back near the Nature Center you can pick up a 1.5-mile loop that visits the ruins of the Estellville Glassworks. The Nature Center and trail guide are among the most informative you will find in New Jersey.

The rich history of this property has created a multitude of surprises awaiting the canine hiker along the trail: an ancient cemetery, ruins from the munitions plant, an artesian well, observation decks in hardwood swamps...

Trail Sense: The trails are well-marked with signposts and maps. You can also find numbered markers on trees throughout the park that are remnants from its days as the South River Game Preserve in the 1940s.

Dog Friendliness
Dogs can hike the trails in Estell Manor Park.

Traffic
These trails receive heavy use from mountain bikers (the park lends them out for free) in addition to hikers and dog walkers.

Canine Swimming
The best place to get your dog some paddling time is in the South River at the end of Artesian Well Road, the park road north of the main park entrance. This also a good parking place to access the trails in the North End.

Trail Time
A good half-day of canine hiking is available here.

There is so much elevated boardwalk through the Atlantic Cedar swamp at Estell Manor that your dog may need a rest to complete it all.

27

Abram S. Hewitt State Forest

The Park

Abram S. Hewitt graduated from Columbia University in 1842 and began teaching in grammar school while he attended law school. He came to tutor Edward Cooper, son of inventor and industrialist, Peter Cooper. Hewitt and young Cooper toured Europe in 1843-1844 and on the return trip their ship wrecked. They survived, their friendship cemented. With Peter Cooper's help the two started a successful ironworks in Trenton and Hewitt married into the Cooper family by wedding Edward's sister. He eventually came into possession of the great ironworks at Ringwood, which Peter Cooper purchased in 1853. In 1867 Hewitt introduced the open-hearth process for manufacturing steel into the United States.

Abram Hewitt's interest in iron began to wane and he became involved in New York politics, winning election to the United States House of Representatives and eventually becoming New York City mayor as part of the progressive movement. He is often called the Father of the New York Subway for his initiatives in public underground transportation, although the subway system wasn't actually built until 10 years after he left office.

Sussex/Passaic

Phone Number
- None

Website
- www.state.nj.us/dep/parksand-forests/parks/abram.html

Admission Fee
- None

Directions
- Take I-287 to Exit 57 and continue on Skyline Drive to its western end at Greenwood Lake Turnpike in Ringwood. Turn right and proceed for 8.4 miles to a Y intersection with Union Valley Road. Take the right fork and continue ahead for 0.3 mile on Warwick Turnpike. Just past a short concrete bridge, there is a turnout on the right side of the road. Park here.

The Walks

The 2,001 acres of Abram S. Hewitt State Forest are accessible only on foot and paw. Most of that walking is done to get to the exposed open rock trails of the Bearfort Ridge. You will need to climb about 600 feet to reach the ridge with its long exposed views of Greenwood Lake and beyond. A common destination is Surprise Lake, which can be circled before the return trip.

Two long-distance trails cross the ridge: the *Appalachian Trail* and the *Highlands Trail*, a 150-mile work-in-progress that will eventually link the Hudson River north of Bear Mountain to the Delaware River.

Puddingstone gives a dog sure footing in the north Jersey mountains.

Trail Sense: There are quite a few marked trails coursing Bearfort Ridge and a trail map can be obtained from the office at Wawayanda State Park, which administers Hewitt Forest.

Dog Friendliness
Dogs are allowed in Hewitt State Forest.
Traffic
Very little.
Canine Swimming
Your dog will come to hike, not swim.
Trail Time
Allow a full day atop Bearfort Ridge.

28
Hartshorne Woods Park

The Park

In 1677, Richard Hartshorne came to the Native Indians with crates of guns, beads and liquor and purchased 2,320 acres that included Sandy Hook on the Atlantic Ocean beach and the land where the park that today carries his name is today. The Lenni Lenape had no idea what land ownership meant, believing that no one could own land any more than anyone could own the sky or sea. But Hartshorne continued to allow access to his new land and managed to settle the area without ever spilling a drop of Indian blood in battle or taking an acre of Indian land without consent.

During World War II, concrete batteries were built as part of the Atlantic Coast Defense System. The military abandoned the facility in the 1970s, and in 1973 Monmouth County purchased 736 acres of wilderness for use as an undeveloped open space.

Monmouth

Phone Number
- (732) 872-0336

Website
- www.monmouthcountyparks.com/parks/hartshorne.asp

Admission Fee
- None

Directions
- Take the Garden State Parkway south to Exit 117. Bear left beyond the toll booths and continue on Route 36 for 11.5 miles. Turn right at the exit for Red Bank Scenic Road, then turn right at the stop sign onto Navesink Avenue. Continue for 0.3 mile to the Buttermilk Valley parking area on the left. To reach Rocky Point continue on Route 36 and turn right on Portland Avenue before crossing the Highlands-SeaBright Bridge and follow to end.

The Walks

Hartshorne Woods is indeed undeveloped, save for its more than 15 miles of trails. In your time here your dog can sample narrow ribbons of dirt, crushed stone access roads and even three miles of paved roads closed to traffic. The park is divided into three segments, each with a feature trail.

From the Buttermilk Valley lot the main loop is the *Laurel Ridge Trail* in the Buttermilk Valley Section, a 2.5-mile romp through - surprise - thick stands of mountain laurel. The center of Hartshorne Woods is the Monmouth Hills Section, disected by the *Grand Tour Trail*. These moderate elevation changes are a welcome find for canine hikers at the shore. In the eastern part of the park

the *Rocky Point Trail* swings through the remains of the old military installation. Short connectors link these main trails to expand your dog's time here.

Trail Sense: There is a trailmap available online and a mapboard at the Buttermilk lot. Trails are also signed at junctions.

Exploring Battery Lewis is part of the canine hiking in Hartshorne Woods.

Dog Friendliness
Dogs are permitted on park trails.

Traffic
Most of the trails attract plenty of mountain bikes and even horses. This is a very busy place - and everyone who fills the parking lots is coming to use the trails in one way or another.

Canine Swimming
On the Rocky Point Trail, a paved road leads down a hill to the Blackfish Cove Fishing Pier. To the left of the pier is a small sandy beach with fantastic canine swimming in the Navesink River.

Trail Time
You can spend a full day here with your dog.

Musconetcong River Reservation

The Park

There are two tracts of land in this park encompassing over 1,100 acres. The Musconetcong Gorge land was originally owned by the Warren Glenn Paper Mill that started production in 1873 and still operates today as Fibermark Inc.

Point Mountain, at 935 feet the third highest spot in Hunterdon County, was added to the park in 1995. The name refers to the prominent crest that the silhouette of the property projects.

The Walks

The *Nature Trail* at the Gorge is a scenic amble that leads into the mossy ravine. It was the result of an Eagle Scout Project and the path is smooth and well-maintained - a joy for any paw. Continue on the *Railroad Trail* for more easy canine hiking but extended time in the Gorge will necessitate a climb to the *Ridge Trail*.

Point Mountain is reached with a steep and rocky scramble up the *Ridge Trail* to the *Overlook Trail*. You can then make a big loop of over two miles to return to the Musconetcong River or retrace your steps back down. Looping around the parking area is the bounding

Hunterdon

Phone Number
- (908) 782-1158

Website
- www.co.hunterdon.nj.us/depts/parks/guides/Musconetcong-Gorge.htm

Admission Fee
- None

Directions
- *For the Gorge*: Travel west on I-78 to Exit 7 and proceed to Route 173 West. Drive 1.3 miles to Route 639. Turn left and travel 4 miles. At the stop sign, bear left on 519, then turn left and cross the Musconetcong River, staying on Route 519. Take the next left onto Dennis Road, a gravel road, and go 0.2 of a mile to the parking area located on the left side of the road.
For Point Mountain: From I-78 take Route 31 for 8 miles north to the traffic light at Asbury-Anderson Road (Route 632). Turn right. Four miles after turning onto Route 632, you will come to a stop sign at the junction with Route 57. Turn right and at the first traffic light, turn right onto Point Mountain Road. The parking area is on the left, a short distance after crossing the bridge.

ing *Riverwalk Trail* that indeed spends plenty of time along the sycamore-edged streamside. This jaunt also has its share of open field canine hiking.

Trail Sense: The trails are blazed and a trail map available.

Dog Friendliness
Dogs are welcome on park trails.

Traffic
There is foot traffic only in the Gorge; horses and bikes can use the trails on Point Mountain but this is not a busy place most days.

Canine Swimming
The Musconetcong River will keep your dog cool.

Trail Time
Several hours to a half-day.

30
Watchung Reservation

The Park

Watchung, from the Lenni Lenape term "Watch Unks" meaning "high hills," Reservation lies at the southern end of a long basaltic ridge that 11,000 years ago was the eastern rim of the 300-square mile glacial remnant, Lake Passaic. East of the Watchung Moutnains the land runs flat to the Atlantic Ocean.

The land was first settled in the 1730s and George Washington took advantage of this natural defensive barrier to twice winter his troops as the British occupied New York City. The Civilian Conservation Corps did work here during the Depression, including planting an impressive pine plantation, and in 1941 the first natural history museum in New Jersey opened on the 2,060-acre preserve.

Today this well-developed park features a riding stable, picnic areas, playgrounds, large open play fields, a greenhouse, trailside museum, scout camp and planetarium. And you can bring your dog too.

The Walks

The beast of the Watchung Reservation trail system is the white-blazed *Sierra Trail* that circles the park for 10 miles, although there are ample opportunities to cut your canine hike short. Overlooks and scenic views are not on the hiking menu but there is a variety of attractions that are not ordinarily expected in such a developed area. Your dog will get a good workout in the ravines and you will pass a cemetery from the 1700s, old mill ruins and several ponds and bubbling streams. The full route utilizes roomy bridle paths and footpaths and does involve several road crossings. There are also several short trail loops near the Trailside Center at the center of the park to sample. All in all, more than you might expect after passing hundreds of people on the drive to the parking lot on a weekend.

Trail Sense: For folks who only feel comfortable in the woods with accurate maps and well-blazed trails, Watchung will not be your first choice. The trail marking can be sporadic and a trail map is a must. One is available in the Trailside Center but not outside and a map can be printed online. Even with a map not all trails are blazed so trust your dog's nose or come prepared to do a bit of wayfinding deduction.

Dog Friendliness
Dogs are allowed to use these trails.

Traffic
This can be a spectacularly busy park but the developed attractions are rather concentrated and deep into the trails you can actually achieve a feeling of being alone with your dog.

Canine Swimming
Lake Surprise, a slender body of water in a depression between ridges is a great place for a dog to swim with its bare dirt banks.

Trail Time
Many hours.

31
Batona Trail

The Park

The *Batona Trail* is a wilderness trail that begins at Ongs Hat to the north and ends at Lake Absegami in Bass River State Forest. The original 30 miles of the Batona Trail were routed and cleared through white cedar and pitch pine forests by volunteers in 1961.

Today the total length of the trail is 50.2 miles with many road crossings that make different lengths of canine hikes possible. The distinctive pink blazes on the Batona Trail were selected by Morris Burdock, then president of the Batona Hiking Club and chief advocate for the building of the trail.

Burlington

Phone Number
- None

Website
- None

Admission Fee
- None

Directions
- The trail runs through Lebanon, Wharton and Bass River State Forests where information on finding a parking lot can be found. Some commonly used starting points are on Routes 563 at Evans Bridge, 542 at Batsto Village at Route 72 at Four Mile.

The Walks

The Batona Trail is easy walking on paw-friendly sand for most of its length. Despite the over-whelming flatness of the surrounding countryside, there are undulating elevation changes on the trail itself. Any dog could walk end to end with no problem, if that was the goal.

The high point on the trail is Apple Pie Hill, soaring 209 feet above sea level (there is a fire tower you can scale - the steps are too open for dogs - and literally scan the east-to-west entirety of New Jersey from Atlantic City to Philadelphia). A superb canine hike is the four-mile walk here from the Carranza Memorial.

For the most part, however, there are no vistas beyond what you see around you - cedar swamps and millions of pine trees. In season wild blueberries and huckleberries can be gobbled along the trail.

Trail Sense: The trail is generously marked with the pink blazes and a five-section trail map is available with a mileage table.

Emilio Carranza Rodriguez was nephew to the founder of the Mexican Air Force, a war hero and his country's greatest aviator. He befriended Charles Lindbergh after the American completed the first solo flight across the Atlantic and then made the second longest non-stop flight from Washington D.C. to Mexico City. Plans were hatched in 1928 for a Mexican capital-to-capital flight. Carranza, then just 22 years old, was selected to make the attempt, carrying the pride of an entire nation in his plane, "The Excelsior."

Haunted by bad weather Carranza was forced to navigate by dead reckoning and came down in an emergency landing in North Carolina.

He continued on to Washington and New York City, where he was feted as a hero for accomplishing the longest flight ever made by a Mexican aviator. Preparations for a return flight to Mexico City were continually delayed until Carranza could wait no longer. On the evening of July 12 he took off in an electrical storm and was never seen alive again. The next day his body was found near the wreckage of his plane, "The Excelsior," in the Pine Barrens where he crashed. Mexican schoolchildren collected pennies to pay for the stone monument that marks the location of his death. Post 11 of the American Legion from Mount Holly, whose members participated in the recovery of the body, still hold a memorial service every year on the second Saturday of July at 1:00 p.m. to honor the memory of Captain Emilio Carranza.

Dog Friendliness

Dogs are allowed to use the Batona Trail.

Traffic

No horses or mountain bikes are allowed on the Batona Trail.

Canine Swimming

The route of the trail is well-lubricated by tea-colored streams and an occasional pond.

Trail Time

Open-ended, up to a full day, or several days.

32
Corson's Inlet State Park

The Park

Corson's Inlet was established in 1969 before every last inch of Jersey shorefront became developed. With its undisturbed sand dune systems and marine estuaries this is one of your last opportunities to experience the Atlantic oceanfront in New Jersey as it was before people discovered the shore.

The Walks

There aren't many places where the hiking public is invited to walk across protected ocean dunes but Corson's Inlet is one. Even rarer still is to find a dune system that permits dogs and again Corson's Inlet is the place - from September 16 through March 31.

Cape May

Phone Number
- (609) 861-2404

Website
- http://www.state.nj.us/dep/parksandforests/parks/corsons.html

Admission Fee
- None

Directions
- The park is located on County Route 619 south of Ocean City and north of Strathmere-Sea Isle City.

The main trail (Yellow) leading away from the small parking lot beside the Rush Chattin Bridge between Ocean City and Strathmere and its two spur paths (Orange, then Red) all lead to the beach that can be used to create loop hikes on the hook-shaped peninsula. All canine hiking is on deep sugar sand and the trails are just long enough to be enjoyable without becoming laborious.

If you come to Corson's Inlet in late September or October on a hot day make sure to bring plenty of fresh water for your dog. Even though the trails aren't long there is little shade among the dunes.

Trail Sense: The trails are blazed but there is no chance of becoming lost in the 98-acre Strathmere Natural Area at Corson's Inlet State Park.

Dog Friendliness

Dogs are welcome at Corson's Inlet anytime except during the nesting season from April 1 to September 15.

Traffic

When the park is busy, dogs aren't permitted anyway. In the off-season you will encounter mostly surf fishermen.

Canine Swimming

Your water-loving dog has a choice here. If the excitement of the Atlantic surf is too intimidating walk around the corner and enjoy the expansive crescent beach along the inlet with its calm, inviting waters.

Trail Time

Depending on how much time you want to spend with your dog on the beach, about an hour.

33

Ken Lockwood Gorge WMA

The Park

Beginning in 1913 Ken Lockwood wrote the outdoors column in the *Newark Evening News*, for most of its 98 years the newspaper of record in New Jersey. "Out In The Open" promoting fishing and hunting, was one of the first of its kind - advocating for the setting aside of public land for wildlife mangement, the stocking of state trout streams and many other practices common in conservation today. A renowned fisherman himself, an artifical streamer fly is named for him. His column ran until his death in 1948.

This 2 1/2-mile section of the South Branch of the Raritan River was purchased by the state in 1948 through what monies raised from the sale of hunting and fishing licenses. Considered one of the prettiest spots in New Jersey, the gorge is an apt memorial to one of the earliest advocates of preserving vanishing wild spaces for the benefit of the public.

Morris

Phone Number
- None

Website
- None

Admission Fee
- None

Directions
- The gorge is east of Route 513 between High Bridge to the south and Califon to the north. From Route 513, take Hoffmans Crossing (about 1.5 miles north of Voorhees State Park) across an iron bridge
- easily spotted from the main road - and make an immediate right on River Road. Continue past several houses to a small parking area at the end of the pavement.

The Walks

This canine hike covers about two miles along the banks of the South Branch, that gets extremely frisky in the gorge. The entire route is on a deeply rutted dirt road that is occasionally braved by a car and also used by cyclists and off-road vehicles. The gorge is not completely straight but twists a bit so you will need to keep a close eye on your dog around bends in the road - admittedly a tough task to take your gaze off the mesmerizing clearn brown-green waters of the riverrrrr of the river and the hemlock-studded gorge. Chances are you won't hear approaching vehicles either as you will be listening to the roaring waters.

Trail Sense: No maps or blazes; follow th road down as far as you like and turn around.

This high bridge across Ken Lockwood Gorge is not the bridge for which the town of High Bridge was named. Your dog can walk across it as part of the Columbia Trail.

Dog Friendliness
Dogs are allowed in the Ken Lockwood Gorge Wildlife Management Area.

Traffic
Vehicular traffic and foot traffic can be heavy on a pretty weekend turning the River Road canine hike into quite a communal experience.

Canine Swimming
This area is for fishermen, supporting a year-round trout fishery. If there isn't a fly fisherman working a deep pool in the river your dog can test the swift-flowing South Branch.

Trail Time
It will take between one and two hours to explore the gorge.

34

Princeton Battlefield State Park

The Park

Having finally achieved an important victory at Trenton in late December 1776, George Washington was in no mood to remain on the western side of the Delaware River. He came back to New Jersey after the new year hoping to surprise the British at Princeton.

His army was spotted at daybreak by an alert British sentry and the Americans were pushed back through a field of frozen cornhusks. Washington, however, counterattacked and chased the British down the road. Major General Cornwallis had hoped to have all of New Jersey under his control by this time but instead had only the ports around New York City.

Mercer

Phone Number
- (609) 921-0074

Website
- http://www.state.nj.us/dep/parksandforests/parks/princeton.html

Admission Fee
- None

Directions
- The park is a little over one mile south of the center of Princeton at 500 Mercer Road (Princeton Pike).

The American Revolution was saved at Trenton and Princeton but little has been done to develop the sites historically. The terrain of the main fighting at the Battle of Princeton has remained virtually unchanged since that pivotal January day in 1777.

The Walks

The explorations on the Princeton Battlefield are around a sloping open field that suggests the terrain on which the armies met. The real canine hiking begins when you slip behind the Clarke House and enter the 588-acre Institute Woods. The trails carve the woodlands into a checkerboard with the first east-west *Trolley Track Trail* marking the route Washington's troops took during the battle. If you hike straight back you'll reach the open paths of the *Cornfield Trail*.

This is easy going for any dog on wide paths of grass and dirt. Look for stands of beech and pine in the woodlands. As you penetrate deeper into the property you reach the Stony Brook that can be crossed for unlimited hiking down the Delaware & Raritan Canal towpath.

Trail Sense: The trails are not marked save for an occasional stone post. There is also no map but the furthest astray you can get is the town of Princeton.

Dog Friendliness

The Institute Woods are private property that has been opened for public use, including dogs.

Traffic

No wheeled vehicles are permitted on these quiet trails.

Canine Swimming

There is access to the Stony Brook.

Trail Time

More than one hour and more are possible.

87

35
Belleplain
State Forest

The Park

Belleplain State Forest was established in 1928 for, as the state says, "recreation, wildlife management, timber production, and water conservation." To achieve these goals, cranberry production in the region just south of the Pine Barrens was the odd man out. During the Great Depression the Civilian Conservation Corps converted Meisle Cranberry Bog into Lake Nummy, the popular recreation area at the center of the Belleplain Forest's 21,034 acres today.

The Walks

Belleplain offers up over 17 miles of non-motorized trails, plus an additional 24 miles of motorized trails if you are

Cape May/Cumberland

Phone Number
- (609) 861-2404

Website
- http://www.state.nj.us/dep/parksandforests/parks/belle.html

Admission Fee
- None

Directions
- The park is roughly situated between major Routes 47 and 49. The park office is on Belleplain-Woodbine Road (Route 550 that connects Route 9 to the east and Belleplain Road (Route 605 to the west).

inclined to dodge the occasional truck or motorcycle. The marquee canine hike for dog lovers is the *East Creek Trail*, a meaty seven-mile loop that connects Lake Nummy to East Creek Pond.

In between the refreshing ponds is level, easy-going for your dog on soft dirt and sand pathways often strewn with pine straw. Expect to hit soupy spots in the trail along the way, although this is more of a hindrance to you than your dog. As you do creative stepping through these mucky areas keep your eyes open for the white blazes to keep going in the right direction.

You will cross active roadways on this trek and to complete the loop you must walk a short distance on busy Route 347. But the shoulder is wide and should be of little consequence to even a skitterish dog.

If you come to Belleplain State Forest with two vehicles, you can use them for shuttle hikes. One such canine hike is along the 2.2-mile *Ponds Trail* that

Bonus

Lying just south of the Pine Barrens, Belleplain enjoys better soil conditions and a correspondingly richer variety of trees. You can enhance your arboreal education with interpretive signs at both the Nature Center and the East Creek Group Cabin.

links East Creek Pond with the Pickle Factory Pond in the southwesternmost part of the forest.

Trail Sense: The trails are energetically blazed and trailheads are well-marked with large signs. A trail map can also be had from the park office and is useful for locating the various trailheads.

Dog Friendliness

Dogs are allowed throughout the forest trails but cannot stay overnight in the campgrounds.

Traffic

Get onto the trails away from the recreation centers and you can rightfully expect to see no one on your canine hike here, especially mid-week or off-season. The usage for each trail is designated so you can avoid horses and bikes if you so choose.

Canine Swimming

The four main ponds in the state forest will set any water-loving dog's tail to wagging.

Trail Time

A complete day's canine hiking is here for the taking.

*Your dog will find the trails in Belleplain Forest
pleasing to the paw indeed.*

36
Lewis Morris County Park

The Park

When it opened in 1958 this was the first park to be created by Morris County in a public park system that now features over 17,000 acres - New Jersey's largest. The original park was 350 acres but has tripled in size over the past half-century.

The park, as is the county, was named in honor of Lewis Morris, a wealthy landowner born near the present-day Bronx in 1671. Morris became a Colonial official and was instrumental in achieving the separation of New Jersey from New York in 1638.

Morris was named the first governor of the State of New Jersey and served until his death in 1646. His family lost all their land and great wealth in New York City during the American Revolution.

Morris

Phone Number
- (973) 829-8257

Website
- www.morrisparks.net/parks/lmmain.htm

Admission Fee
- No

Directions
- Take I-287 into Morristown. From Morristown Green turn right onto Washington Street. Go 3.5 miles west towards Mendham and Chester on Route 510 West/Route 24. The park entrance is on the left.

The Walks

With six picnic areas, a recreational lake, a group camping area and several ballfields most people don't think "hiking" when they think about Lewis Morris County Park. But there are many miles of woodsy trails that leave all the recreational amenities behind. The terrain is hilly but never taxing - many of the trails slide around the hills rather than charge right up them. There is little understory and the airy woods give this canine hike a big feel.

Parking in the Mendham Overlook Area provides central access to the trail system. The *Green Trail* and *Red Trail* are connected loops that are more or less surrounded by the *Yellow Trail*. They all explore the same ridges and valley so it is no problem to bounce back and forth. If your dog is having too good a time to return to the car there are connectors to the *Grand Loop* and hours more walking in Morristown National Historical Park.

Trail Sense: A detailed trail map is available and the trails are reliably blazed.

Dog Friendliness
Dogs are allowed on the Lewis Morris trails.

Traffic
The trails are multi-use but not as crowded as other parts of the park.

Canine Swimming
In the off-season when no one is around Sunrise Lake can make a fine canine swimming pool but there is no swimming along the trails.

Trail Time
More than one hour.

Your dog is bound to love the roomy trails at Lewis Morris Park.

37
South Mountain Reservation

The Park

In 1895 Essex County began buying land that would become South Mountain Reservation. They retained Central Park creator Frederick Law Olmsted to design the new park. Olmsted was in the twilight of his career, about to turn the business over to his sons, but surveyed the property and declared it one of the choicest park sites he had ever seen. It was the first of more than two dozen projects the Olmsteds would design for Essex County.

South Mountain has remained in its wild state. Working from Olmsted site plans the Civilian Conservation Corps built trails, bridges and picnic shelters in the 1930s. Today's park is the largest in the Essex County Park Commission system at 2,047.14 acres, to be exact.

Essex

Phone Number
- None

Website
- None

Admission Fee
- No

Directions
- From I-78 take Exit 50 and head north on Millburn Avenue to Brookside Drive and the park. To reach the trail to Washington Rock, turn right on Brookside, right on South Orange Avenue and right on Washington Rock Drive to parking area.

The Walks

Water is the star at South Mountain. The Rahway River makes a pleasant canine hiking companion and there are cascades and even a 25-foot plunge over bare basalt rock to enjoy. You'll get an occasional steep ascent but most of the going on South Mountain trails will be easily devoured by any dog. Crest Drive has been closed to vehicular traffic and makes a pleasant start to an outing here, either on the curling roadway or an adjacent footpath with Washington Rock the most common destination.

Beyond Lookout Point, much of your day will be spent on the yellow-blazed *Lenape Trail* with a return on the white-blazed *Rahway Trail*. This loop will take the better part of two hours with much more available. The footpath can be challenging with rocky footing and stream crossings and you will notice most folks are keeping to the gravel roads in the reservation.

Trail Sense: There is nothing at the parking lot to guide you here whatsoever. The trails are blazed once you stumble onto the trailheads but where do they go? First-timers are best advised to follow the closed Crest Drive to Washington Rock (on a busy day follow the crowds) and then decide how bold you feel about further explorations. Anything beyond the yellow-to-white trail route will be a calculated adventure. The county claims there are 27 miles of carriage roads and 19 miles of hiking and walking trails. Bon chance.

Dog Friendliness
Dogs are allowed to use these trails.
Traffic
Many of the gravel paths are used by mountain bikers and the park will be crowded until you get deep into the trails.
Canine Swimming
There are ponds and streams along the trail aplenty for your water-loving dog.
Trail Time
Many, many hours.

38
Cheesequake State Park

The Park

Located between northern and southern plant communities, this area has long been recognized for its botanical value. The State of New Jersey began acquiring land for the park in 1938 and opened a picnic grove and hiking trails two years later.

The name Cheesequake is commonly believed to derive from a Lenni Lenape Indian term roughly translating to "upland village." But the area does rest atop a tetonic fault and one of the earliest earthquakes on record that shook the metropolitan New York area in 1779 was centered in Cheesequake.

Middlesex

Phone Number
- (732) 566-2161

Website
- www.state.nj.us/dep/park-sandforests/parks/cheese-quake.html

Admission Fee
- No

Directions
- From the Garden State Parkway take Exit 120 and follow signs for the park through residential streets.

The Walks

The agreeable canine hiking at Cheesequake State Park is concentrated in the western section of its 1,274 acres. Four trails all launch from the same trailhead just past the park entrance. Another trail designed for mountain bike use but open to foot traffic is also available hard by the Garden State Parkway.

The star trek here is along the *Green Trail* that will introduce your dog to just about every forest type in New Jersey - scrub pine barrens, Atlantic white cedar swamp, red maples in saltwater marshes and upland hardwood forests. There is just enough elevation changes to keep your dog interested on these paw-friendly trails.

Trail Sense: A detailed park map is available and a trail guide can be found at the office. If you arrive at the trailhead empty-handed you can study a well-drawn mapboard.

Dog Friendliness
Dogs are permitted on park trails but not overnight in the campground.
Traffic
The compact trail system can seem more crowded than it actually is.
Canine Swimming
The *Yellow Trail* drops down to Hooks Creek Lake for a quick chance at a doggie dip.
Trail Time
More than one hour.

39
Tourne County Park

The Park

Tourne, roughly translated from Dutch as "mountain" or "overlook," is the last remaining undeveloped chunk of land from the Great Boonton Tract that was purchased by David Ogden, Colonial Attorney-General of New Jersey, in 1759. This was a mining area and McCaffrey Lane that runs into the park was designed in 1767 to haul iron ore from Hibernia's mines to the Ogden ironworks in Old Boonton.

Clarence Addington DeCamp owned most of the land that is now Tourne Park in the first half of the 20th century. With just hand tools and levers, DeCamp - a conservationist before there was such a term - built two roads to the top of the hill for people to enjoy the views. Morris County came into possession of the land after DeCamp's passing and opened the 545-acre park for the public in 1960.

Morris

Phone Number
- (973) 326-7631

Website
- www.morrisparks.net/parks/tournemain.htm

Admission Fee
- No

Directions
- From I-80 take Exit 38 for Denville. Follow Route 46 east through Denville to Mountain Lakes. Turn right onto the Boulevard and go through Mountain Lakes. Bear left onto Powerville Road. Take the first left onto McCaffrey Lane to the park.

The Walks

The must-do canine hike at Tourne County Park is the 370-foot climb to the 897-foot namesake summit. Your dog will be using the same roads that Clarence DeCamp carved a century ago (*the DeCamp Trail*). The wide path can be a bit rocky on your dog's paws but it is only a two-mile round trip. There are views in every direction by the time you crest the summit and head down the opposite side.

After conquering the Tourne most people return to their cars and leave. Don't be too quick to follow their lead. Across the road the *Hemlock Trail* is a sporty push up a hill under exceedingly pleasant woodlands. The trail system here also meanders along Rigby's Brook in airy woods. More blazed foot trails can be found for your dog in the western areas of the park; what they lack in views they compensate for in elbow room.

Trail Sense: A detailed trail map is available and the route to the Tourne is indicated by signs.

Dog Friendliness
Dogs are not allowed in the *Wildflower Trail* area.

Traffic
Everybody can make the trek to the top of the Tourne and there is usually a steady stream of folks on the trail. But cross McCaffrey Lane and you could well spend your canine hiking day alone.

Canine Swimming
Rigby's Brook is a great stream for splashing but not deep enough for dog paddling.

Trail Time
More than one hour.

Dogs have been climbing the Tourne for over a century to enjoy the views - many years before it was a park.

40
Washington Crossing State Park

The Park

These sleepy, tree-lined banks along the Delaware River became immortalized in American mythology on the icy night of December 25, 1776 when General George Washington led a demoralized Continental Army across the river to score a surprise victory over unsuspecting Hessian troops in Trenton.

Land was eventually preserved on both the New Jersey and Pennsylvania sides of the river to commemorate one of the turning points in the battle for independence.

Mercer

Phone Number
- (609) 737-0623

Website
- www.state.nj.us/dep/
forestry/parks/washcros.htm

Admission Fee
- None

Directions
- From I-95, take Route 29 north. Parking is available along the Delaware River just past Route 546.

The Walks

There are dog-walking opportunities on both sides of the Delaware; the more historic explorations can be found on the Pennsylvania side, the more natural trails in New Jersey. Quiet paths meander through an historic village at the scene of the American disembarkment in Washington's Crossing Historic Park.

On the New Jersey side, the terrain instantly becomes rolling and wooded beyond the Johnson Ferry House where the troops landed in what is now Washington Crossing State Park. The many miles of trails are carved through a mixed hardwood and spruce forest, often times plunging into and out of wide ravines.

Washington Crossing State Park can also be used as a jumping off point for hikes up and down the towpath along the 70-mile Delaware and Raritan Canal.

Trail Sense: The trails are not blazed and maps are not available.

Dog Friendliness
Dogs can enjoy the New Jersey trails and on the Pennsylvania side look at the outside of buildings in Washington Crossing Historic Park's McConkey's Ferry Section. Dogs are not allowed in Bowman's Hill Wildflower Preserve upstream in the Thompson's Mill Section on the Pennsylvania side.

Traffic
The towpath is popular with joggers and bicyclists but the crowds thin out on the hills of the state park.

Canine Swimming
There is no good access to the Delaware River at this point.

Trail Time
More than an hour, especially if you set off on the towpath.

*"The greatest pleasure of a dog is that you may make a fool
of yourself with him, and not only will he not scold you,
but will make a fool of himself too."*

- Samuel Butler

41

Brendan T. Byrne State Forest

The Park

It is hard to imagine this vast 32,000-acre forest stripped barren as it was a little more than a century ago. The Lebanon Glass Works set up shop in 1851 and within 16 years had felled every stick of timber for miles in every direction. With its supply of wood depleted the furnace was shut down and abandoned. The state began buying the land that ultimately became Lebanon State Forest in 1908 (and Brendan T. Byrne State Forest a century later) and once again the sandy soil is blanketed with vibrant stands of pine, oak, maple, gum and Atlantic white cedar.

Burlington

Phone Number
- (609) 08064

Website
- www.state.nj.us/dep/forestry/parks/lebanon.htm

Admission Fee
- None

Directions
- The Brendan Byrne State Forest is accessible by State Highway Routes 70 and 72.

The Walks

If you are not in the mood for hours and hours of flat, level walking where the view seldom changes, do not bring the dog to Brendan T. Byrne State Forest. Of course, a closer look will reveal such treasures as rare orchids and carniverous plants and the easy-walking soft trails are ideal for any dog.

Ongs Hat, at the western tip of the park, is the northern terminus for the *Batona Trail* and about 9 miles of the 49-mile route slice across the lower edge of the state forest. The Batona can be used to create large canine hiking loops with other forest trails.

Another good walking choice is the *Cranberry Trail* which runs 5 miles to Pakim Pond. Pakim Pond, from the Lenni-Lenape word for "cranberry" was once used as a reservoir for an adjacent cranberry bog, now a swamp.

For the more adventurous canine hiker there are over 20 miles of wilder-ness trails and if your restless spirit is still not sated it is easy to get off the grid here: Brendan T. Byrne State Forest features 400 miles of unpaved roads. The trails are almost uniformly soft and easy on the paw.

Trail Sense: If you spend any time at all in Brendan T. Byrne State Forest you will get lost. A park map marks major trails and roads and hold on tight for orientation. If it's hot make sure you have plenty of drinking water and insect repellent.

Dog Friendliness

Dogs are permitted on trails throughout the forest but are not allowed in the campgrounds.

Traffic

If you are looking to lose yourself with your dog in nature, this is the place.

Canine Swimming

The terrain is pocked with small ponds and creeks that make for superb swimming holes.

Trail Time

Many, many hours if so desired.

Your dog can go all day on the flat, paw-friendly trails of sand and pine straw in the Sand Barrens.

42

Gateway National Recreation Area
– Sandy Hook Unit

The Park

Sandy Hook is a 7-mile sand spit dangling into the Atlantic Ocean off the northern tip of New Jersey. Ships sailing into New York harbor have always needed to navigate around the shifting sands of Sandy Hook. The first lighthouse was built from lottery funds in 1764. The strategic peninsula has been fortified since the War of 1812 and the Hook was the site of the first United States Army Proving Ground. The last active military base, Fort Hancock, closed in 1974 but the United States Coast Guard still maintains an active presence at Sandy Hook.

Monmouth

Phone Number
- (732) 872-5970

Website
- http://www.nps.gov/gate/

Admission Fee
- Yes, in summer.

Directions
- Sandy Hook is located off Route 36 near the town of Highlands.

The Walks

The best canine hiking in the 1,655-acre Sandy Hook Unit is on the seven miles of ocean beach. The open sands of North Beach curl around to reveal views of the Brooklyn skyline and the Verrazano Narrows Bridge, the longest suspension bridge in the world when it opened in 1964.

Open all year to dogs are short nature trails through a 264-acre maritime forest that holds the greatest concentration of American Holly on the East Coast. When hiking around sand trails, steer your dog clear of low-lying prickly pear cacti that grow in abundance on the peninsula.

In addition to the unspoiled natural areas at Sandy Hook, there are plenty of places to explore with your dog through historic Fort Hancock, much of which is used for educational purposes today. Interpretive trails describe missile testing sites, anti-aircraft defenses, and lead into overgrown gun batteries.

Trail Sense: A park map is available.

Dog Friendliness

Dogs are not allowed in the recreation area from March 15 to Labor Day to protect nesting shorebirds. Dogs are also not allowed on the *Old Dune Trail*.

Traffic

The off-season is a joy with little competition on the beach.

Canine Swimming

As much Atlantic Ocean time as your dog wants.

Trail Time

You can easily make a day of it on the beaches of Sandy Hook.

43

Allamuchy Mountain State Park

The Park

Most of the 8,000+ acres that comprise Allamuchy Mountain State Park were once the estate of Rutherford Stuyvesant - a direct descendant of Peter Stuyvesant, the last governor of Dutch New Amsterdam. He established a 1000-acre game preserve here and introduced the English pheasant to America. The State of New Jersey purchased the land in the 1970s.

The name comes from the Lenni Lenape Indians who lived here half a millenium ago. The chief of this particular settlement was Allamuchahokkingen and the first European settlement in 1715 was named for him. After friends and relatives got tired of writing that on mailing envelopes the name was shortened to Allamucha.

Sussex/Warren

Phone Number
- None

Website
- www.nj.gov/dep/parksandfor-ests/parks/allamuch.html

Admission Fee
- None

Directions
- From I-80 take Exit 19 and head south on Route 517, following the signs for Stephens State Park.
Go two miles looking for a small sign (maybe) and an unimproved road on the left that passes through some houses to a clearing that doubles as a parking lot.
If you care to challenge a rugged dirt road you can access lots deeper into the park.

The Walks

It's a beautiful day in central New Jersey and you want to go for a long hike with your dog but you don't want to spend the day dodging other trail users. Where do you go? Allamuchy Mountain State Park. Even though the park abuts busy I-80 few people are familiar with it. The State of New Jersey is in no hurry to rectify the situation. The park is undeveloped, save for a trail system, and lacks signage. Even when you are there, there is nothing to tell you that you are there, to paraphrase Gertrude Stein's summation of her Oakland past.

The Allamuchy Natural Area is crisscrossed by about 15 miles of trails, some multi-use roads, others footpaths. Allamuchy Mountain is flat-topped so you are never really climbing although the terrain certainly varies. There are no great destinations here - Deer Park Pond in the center of the property makes a worthy focal point. This is just a place to come and hike with your dog, ducking in and out of attractive, expansive woodlands and two dozen succession fields in various states of growth to established hardwood forests.

If you really want to disappear with your dog there are another 25 miles of unmarked trails across I-80 in the northern chunk of the park. This trail system is accessed on Waterloo Road, where the parking lot is the southern terminus for the 21-mile *Sussex Branch Trail*.

Trail Sense: There is a reasonably accurate park map and the trails are blazed. But the blazed colors seem to have been re-done and don't match the map colors. Still, you should be able to navigate your way around.

Dog Friendliness
Dogs are permitted on all these park trails.
Traffic
Most trails are open to mountain bikes and horses but if the sight of perhaps one bike an hour is enough to spoil your day you can head off on some hiker-only trails.
Canine Swimming
There is fine dog paddling in Deer Park Pond.
Trail Time
As much as a full day of canine hiking.

"Happiness is dog-shaped."
-Chapman Pincher

44
Shark River Park

The Park

The wetlands and floodplains of the Shark River were the site of Monmouth County's first park, created in 1961. Shark River's 588 acres are neatly divided into a recreational area that attracts picnickers and fishermen and ice skaters and an isolated trail system of almost seven miles.

The Walks

The *Hidden Creek Trail* loops the trail system and visits most of the diverse landscapes packed into Shark River Park. The passage is surprisingly undulating although terms like "moderate" and even "challenging" used by the park to describe trails here is a bit of a stretch. Your dog will enjoy these packed sand and dirt paths through a dense mixed forest.

The out-and-back *Pine Hills Trail* provides a sporty detour into some of the deeper undulations in the park and the *Rivers Edge Trail* drops into the floodplain to twist along the Shark River for the better part of a mile. This is not the Shark River of a few miles downstream at the Atlantic Ocean with marinas and open water. At this point the fast-flowing water can just about be stepped across and carries a strange industrial-hued tint.

Trail Sense: There is a trailmap available at the trailhead and the trails are marked with signs and geometric markers. Even so stay alert when the trail meanders across transition areas of the park.

Monmouth

Phone Number
- (732) 922-4080

Website
- www.monmouthcountyparks.com/parks/shark_park.asp

Admission Fee
- None

Directions
- From the Garden State Parkway take Exit 100 (Route 33 East). At Schoolhouse Road turn right and follow to the park. The main trail system is across the road from the parking lot.

Dog Friendliness

Dogs are permitted in Shark River Park.

Traffic

The trails are multi-use with bicycles and horse traffic.

Canine Swimming

If no one has a fishing line in the small lake, this is a fine canine swimming hole. The Shark River occasionally pools deep enough for brief dog paddling.

Trail Time

More than one hour.

45
Kittatinny Valley State Park

The Park

Fred Hussey's family made their money in whaling in early America. In the mid 1900s Hussey owned a company called Aeroflex that developed an ingenious rubber camera mount that was the first way to take steady photograhs from the air. The company started by producing aerial maps but the camera mount was invaluable to the military in identifying targets for bombing raids.

In the late 1950s Hussey built an airport here to maintain his private collection of WWI aircraft, antique cars, and military surplus cars. For its time, the facility was state-of-the-art; almost everything was custom-built.

Sussex

Phone Number
- (973) 786-6445

Website
- www.state.nj.us/dep/park-sandforests/parks/kittval.html

Admission Fee
- Yes, during summer in the recreation area

Directions
- From I-80, take Route 206 north for 8 miles through Andover Borough. Turn right onto Goodale Road and follow it to the park entrance on the right.

Bonus
The long, gentle grades of the Sussex Branch Trail and the Paulinskill Valley Trail are ideal for dog sledding in the winter. Check with the park for any scheduled events or bring your own team.

After his death in the mid-1970s, the LoRae family acquired the land in an auction and converted several buildings into stables to house their beloved Arabian horses.

The State of New Jersey acquired the property in 1994 and created Kittatinny Valley State Park. The airport still operates today under the New Jersey Forest Fire Service. It is the only state-owned and operated airport in New Jersey. The former Hussey home on Lake Aeroflex has been converted into the new park Visitor Center.

The Walks

Just about any type of canine hike your dog is after can be crafted in Kittatinny Valley State Park. The *Sussex Branch Trail*, the remnants of the Sussex Branch Line of the Erie-Lackawanna Railroad, runs down the spine of the park providing relaxed, peaceful trotting on cinder-based paths moving on mild grades. It can be used to create hiking loops of varying lengths.

For a more energetic pace there are miles of short, interlaced trails that roll on small hills through woods and around rock outcroppings. Four lakes are a prominent feature of Kittatinny Valley State Park but the trails just tap the water occasionally.

Trail Sense: There is a park map available that provides a general picture of the trail system; there are some color blazes on the trails but they don't correspond to anything on the map.

Dog Friendliness
Dogs are permitted on park trails.
Traffic
There is healthy competition from mountain bikes on these trails and local clubs perform trail maintenance for bikes. The trails on the western side of the Sussex Branch Trail are open to hunting.
Canine Swimming
There are boat ramps at two ponds that are the best bet for a doggie swim.
Trail Time
More than one hour.

46
Allaire
State Park

The Park

James Peter Allaire was born in Nova Scotia in 1785 where his family, loyal to the crown of King George III, fled in exile during the American Revolution. The Allaires returned to New York City in 1806 and the 21-year old James Allaire opened a brass foundry.

He also was a keen enough inventor to patent a dramatic improvement for steam boilers and from 1816 to 1840 he operated the largest marine engine building shop in the United States.

In 1822 Allaire came to the wilds of New Jersey and bought the 5,000-acre Monmouth Furnace to supply his engine works. The isolation of his new Howell Works caused him to build a self-sufficient village around

Monmouth

Phone Number
- (732) 938-2371

Website
- www.state.nj.us/dep/park-sandforests/parks/allaire.html

Admission Fee
- Yes, Memorial Day to Labor Day but for trail use you can park outside the main lot.

Directions
- From the Garden State Parkway take Exit 98 and follow the well-marked signs to the park. From I-195 use Exit 31B.

it. The ironworks thrived until 1850 when Allaire retired. He lived out his last years at the site and the property remained in the Allaire family until 1901.

Legendary newspaper editor Arthur Brisbane bought the property as a retreat and maintained much of the old village. His estate deeded 800 acres to the State of New Jersey and the park today covers more than 3,000 acres.

The Walks

Thanks to the Manasquan River the trail system is a bit disjointed; to reach all of it you need to drive to various parking lot trailheads on either side of the water. From the parking area at the Allaire Village you can access a 4.5-mile walking trail that tours the historic buildings and joins up with the stacked loop *Red Trail* at the Nature Center. The *Yellow Trail* slips out of the village and explores the Manasquan River floodplain. The canine hiking is easy on these wide, pedestrian-only trails and the pace is relaxed away from the village.

Allaire State Park is laced with sand roads and an abandoned railroad have been converted into a multi-use trail. Jump on any of these well-marked pathways for hours more of comfortable canine hiking in the northernmost reaches of the Pine Barrens.

Trail Sense: A trail map is available and the trails are blazed and signed.

Dog Friendliness
Dogs are permitted on park trails but not overnight in the campground.

Traffic
The multi-use trails are designed for horses - that can be rented in the park. Trails in the day use area are for foot traffic only.

Canine Swimming
The Manasquan River is about 30 feet wide but only averages about two feet deep.

Trail Time
Several hours to half a day.

"We are alone, absolutely alone on this chance planet; and, amid all the forms of life that surround us, not one, excepting the dog, has made an alliance with us."
-Maurice Maeterlinck

47
Tatum Park

The Park

Charles Tatum was a prominent glass manufacturer with factories in Keyport and Millville. He selected this land as a summer home in 1905 and his family continued to farm 170 acres here until 1973. A portion of the farm was then donated to Monmouth County and additional acreaged has since been acquired to fatten the current park size to 368 acres.

The Walks

Tatum Park serves up as nice a mix of open field and mixed-hardwood canine hiking as you are liable to find in New Jersey. You can start your explorations from either the Holland Activity Center or the Red Hill Activity Center but the centrally located Holland Center offers a greater variety of canine hiking options.

Monmouth

Phone Number
- (732) 671-1987

Website
- www.monmouthcountyparks. com/parks/tatum.asp

Admission Fee
- No

Directions
- Take Exit 114 from the Garden State Parkway onto Red Hill Road heading east. You can continue to the Red Hill Activity Center ahead on your left but the better choice is to head for the Holland Activity Center by turning left on Van Schoick Road and right on Holland Road to the entrance on the right.

Two parallel trails lead away from the parking lot. If you want to start your dog with a jaunt down old farm roads and through blossoming meadows start off down the *Tatum Ramble Trail* and pick up the *Meadow Run Trail* for a three-mile easy loop. The other choice, the Indian Springs Trail is another old road that once served as the main entrance to the farm. It will eventually lead to the twisting *Dogwood Hollow Trail* or the *Holly Grove Trail* - both narrow, rolling dirts paths through thriving woodlands.

Trail Sense: A trail map is available at the trailhead.

Dog Friendliness
Dogs are welcome and poop bags are provided.

Traffic
This is a relatively uncrowded place, especially on weekdays; many of the cars in the lot will be here for the many park programs and not necessarily trail use. The Holly Grove Trail and Dogwood Hollow Trail are for foot traffic only. The rest of the trails are open to horses and bikes.

Canine Swimming
Your dog can splash in some old farm ponds or slender streams in the hollows of the park but little more.

Trail Time
More than one hour.

"If you pick up a starving dog and make him prosperous,
he will not bite you; that is the principal
difference between a dog and a man."
                                        -Mark Twain

48
Schooley's Mountain County Park

The Park

The quiet, spacious woods and cloistered waterfalls on Schooley's Mountain belie a very active past. Stone has been quarried here to build area houses. The iron ore ripped from the ground was so magnetic the workers could not use metal tools to extract it. The pent-up power of the rushing waterfalls was tapped to generate electricity. Before that, in the early 1800s, Joseph Heath had opened a spa and touted the waters as the purest in America, able to heal whatever was ailing you. Folks came in stagecoaches and then railroads to take the waters. After the spa came a boarding school, then a YMCA camp. Through it all the mountain retained the name of the Schooley family who lived here in the 1700s.

Morris County acquired the land in 1968 and opened the 797-acre park, mostly on wooded hillsides, in 1974.

Morris

Phone Number
- (973) 962-7031

Website
- www.morrisparks.net/parks/schooleysmain.htm

Admission Fee
- None

Directions
- Take I-80 West to I-287 South and Exit 22. Go north on Route 206 to the Route 24 intersection. Turn left onto Route 24, heading west up Schooley's Mountain, past Washington Township Municipal Building. Turn right at park sign onto Camp Washington Road. Continue on same, which becomes Springtown Road, to the park on the right side.

The Walks

Rarely will a canine hike turn as wild and wooly as fast as the one at Schooley's Mountain. Just minutes past starting out at the lodge and easing down well- maintained wooden steps by the lodge and stepping through the serenity of a forested oudoor chapel you and your dog are traipsing past waterfalls and scrambling across boulders as the trail seems to disappear. You are just yards from the roadway and neighborhoods but you may as well have descended into the wilderness of the early 1700s when all this land was just referred to as The Great Forest.

After exploring the Electric Brook gorge soon enough your dog is trudging uphill on a somewhat rocky road that will eventually lead to scrambled boulder fields and overlooks of the countryside. The excitement now gears down as the rest of your dog's outing is spent on old roads and footpaths under an attractive forest. The loop to return to Lake George covers about two miles.

Electric Creek gets your canine hike at Schooley's Mountain off to a rollicking start.

Patriot's Path also slices over Schooley's Mountain. You can use this long-distance trail to cut off the blue-blazed loop or, if your dog is really enjoying her time on Schooley's Mountain, pick your way through the boulders and hike down off the mountain.

Trail Sense: There is a mapboard at the lodge parking lot but nothing to carry with you. It can get confusing as the blazes disappear some times and intertwine at others. Trails run down either side of Electric Brook but the one on the road side of the stream deadends until a bridge is repaired.

Dog Friendliness
Dogs are allowed on Schooley's Mountain.

Traffic
Mostly other hikers; once you put Lake George behind you the woods become your own on most days.

Canine Swimming
If there are no fishermen or swimmers, there is access to Lake George.

Trail Time
More than one hour.

49
Bass River
State Forest

The Park

When Governor Edward Stokes instigated the purchase of 597 acres of woodlands along the Bass River in 1905, New Jersey had its first state forest.

The Civilian Conservation Corps set up camp in the forest in 1933 and stayed for a decade building roads, bridges and various shelters and cabins. They also impounded two streams to create 67-acre Lake Absegami, the park's feature attraction.

The Walks

Although the Bass River State Forest covers 26,700 acres, the marked trails are all short and are centered at the park office. The feature trail is the one-mile *Absegami Trail* that winds through a small Atlantic white cedar bog. Some of this trip is across a wooden boardwalk.

Some of the best canine hiking is across the street from the park office on the *Pink* and *Green* trails. These adjacent loops, partly on wide sand roads, travel beneath thick pines for 2.2 and 3.2 miles, respectively. This is easy going for your dog on soft surfaces. - but the pines don't smother all the traffic noise from adjacent Garden State Parkway.

The Bass River State Forest is also the southern terminus for the pink-blazed *Batona Trail* that runs through Wharton State Forest and Byrne State Forest for 50 miles. The wilderness path through the Pine Barrens was begun in 1961 and fully linked the three state forests in 1987.

Trail Sense: Canine hikers are told that "all trails leave from the parking lot across from Lake Absegami. Now, at some trail systems this means multiple trailheads at a centralized location. At Bass River it means that a single trail

Burlington/Ocean

Phone Number
- (609) 296-1114

Website
- http://www.state.nj.us/dep/parksandforests/parks/bass.html

Admission Fee
- Entrance fee charged Memorial Day to Labor Day.

Directions
- The state forest is six miles west of Tuckerton on Stage Road. From the Garden State Parkway South take Exit 52 or North take Exit 50 and follow brown signs.

will eventually lead to various trailheads. Once this is cleared up, navigation becomes a bit easier. The trails are not blazed but are marked with signposts and a sketched-out trail map is available.

Dog Friendliness
Dogs are allowed on the trails but not in the campgrounds overnight.
Traffic
If you come to hike with your dog and not use the lake you will find little competition for the trails. Bring your dog in the off-season and you can expect a private forest.
Canine Swimming
The trails don't lead to any swimming opportunities although Lake Absegami is a prime doggie swimming hole in the off-season.
Trail Time
Several hours - or much more if you set off on the Batona Trail.

50
Double Trouble State Park

The Park

Sawmills have long operated at this site on the Cedar Creek, processing dense stands of Atlantic White Cedar into shingles and shipmasts. Over time cranberries were planted in the swamps vacated by the harvested trees.

In 1909 the entire area became the Double Trouble Cranberry Company. The name supposedly comes from problems with the dams used to sustain the bogs. One theory has two wash-outs in a single spring rainy season inspiring the name and another traces it to two separate leaky holes gnawed in a dam by muskrats.

Today the park centers around Double Trouble Historic Village, a cluster of 14 surviving structures from the late 1800s.

Ocean

Phone Number
- (732) 341-6662

Website
- http://www.state.nj.us/dep/parksandforests/parks/double.html

Admission Fee
- None

Directions
- Traveling south on the Garden State Parkway take Exit 80 and turn left to Double Trouble Road. Follow to end in about four miles and cross the road into the park. Heading north use Exit 77 and turn left to park entrance in 1/4 mile.

The Walks

The park preserves more than 8,000 acres of natural Pine Barrens habitat but you will experience just a tiny slice of it on just a single trail in Double Trouble State Park. The 1.5-mile *Nature Trail* leaves on an old sand road along a series of cranberry bogs. You leave the open area around the ponds with a sharp right turn into a dark avenue of Atlantic Cedar. The trees were once thought to be limitless in the Pinelands when the sawmills were running full steam.

In time you'll reach more bogs and complete your canine hiking loop on more sand roads and across Cedar Creek and back into the village. You and your dog have now experienced what lies beyond in millions of acres of the Pine Barrens in a short, exceedingly pleasant outing.

Trail Sense: A park map exists but isn't always in the box at the trailhead that begins at the restored cranberry packing house. There are signs that guide you along but if you take your dog out into the spiderweb of Pinelands sand roads beyond the Nature Trail you are on your own.

Dog Friendliness
Dogs are allowed throughout the park.
Traffic
Double Trouble State Park receives a light to moderate visitation.
Canine Swimming
When not choked with berries your dog can jump into a bog; poke around a bit and you can find access to the ultra pure waters of Cedar Creek.
Trail Time
The nature trail takes about 45 minutes to complete - of course you can duck down a sand road and disappear in the Pine Barrens with your dog for days.

*This isn't a giant agility course for dogs.
It is the Nature Trail as it passes through
an Atlantic cedar swamp.*

51
Mills Reservation

The Park

A gift of 119 acres from the Davella Mills Foundation in 1954 got the ball rolling for this greenspace in heavily suburbanized Cedar Grove-Montclair. The original donation stipulated the hillsides be kept in a natural state and the only development - no buildings at all - at Mills Reservation are three miles of curving paths designed by the Olmsted family. Their minimally intrusive design was the last of many projects the historic landscape archtitecture firm did for Essex County.

The Walks

If you are seeking a communal canine hike, Mills Reservation is your place to come in New Jersey. The parking lots fill early and having a dog in tow almost seems a requirement to use

Essex

Phone Number
- None

Website
- www.last-exit.net/essexcounty/index.php?section=dept/p/mi

Admission Fee
- None

Directions
- Take Exit 151 off the Garden State Parkway onto Watchung Avenue in Montclair and head west. Continue to the end at Upper Mountain Avenue and turn right. Turn left in 1.7 miles at Normal Avenue to entrance on the left. Parking is also available on Edgecliff Road for a handful of cars.

the trails. Although you are squeezed into housing developments on every side these wooded trails do manage to radiate an air of the great outdoors.

Most folks are trekking on wide, crushed-gravel paths that roll easily around the hills but narrow ribbons of dirt can provide some relief. There are no navigation aids and most likely you will bang into a residential street at a park boundary at some point. Keep at the trails, however, until you reach a flat rock outcrop at Quarry Point with its views of migratory birds and eastern New Jersey.

Trail Sense: These trails are blazed but without any park map their purpose doesn't reveal itself to the uninitiated visitor.

This is the only structure your dog will find at Mills Reservation.

Dog Friendliness

This is the park where area dogs come to run.

Traffic

The wide paths are attractive for strolling and on a sunny day expect the park to be filled with neighborhood families.

Canine Swimming

None.

Trail Time

About one hour.

52

Holmdel Park

The Park

The land here was first cleared for subsitence farmin around the time of the American Revolution. In 1806 Hendrick Longstreet, who would become quite a land baron in Monmouth County, pieced together several small farms totalling 495 acres.

While much of what was grown here was used on Longstreet Farm potatoes were a cash crop. The farm remained in family hands until it was bought by the county in 1962. A small part of Longstreet Farm has been preserved as a living history history farm, interpreting rural life in the 1890s.

The Walks

Canine hikers visiting Holmdel Park will want to drive past Longstreet Farm and turn right and head up the hill to Parking Lot 3, which is at the center of the trail system. The trails are a series of loops, most around one ile, that you can use to build a canine hiking day. The terrain is hilly but the trails work around the slopes rather than pushing up the hill.

Added up, there are eight miles of trails through beech, hickory, oak, tulip, spruce and pine trees. There is a not much understory in this agriculture field-turned forest so you get a big feel to these dog walks. The most demanding canine hike in the park is the Cross-Country Trail that circles the property for 3.1 miles and delivers all the undulations at Holmdel.

Trail Sense: A detailed trail map is available and it is needed to identify locations of trailheads and junctions.

Monmouth

Phone Number
- (732) 872-2670

Website
- www.monmouthcountyparks.com/parks/holmdel.asp

Admission Fee
- No

Directions
- From the Garden State Parkway take Exit 114 onto Red Hill Road west to Crawfords Corner Road. Turn right and follow signs to Holmdel Park on Longstreet Road. From Route 34, take Roberts Road. Turn left onto Longstreet Road.

Dog Friendliness
Dogs are not allowed in Longstreet Farm but can hike the park trails.

Traffic
This large 564-acre park supports plenty of visitors and the hills aren't intimidating enough to keep folks off the trails.

Canine Swimming
Small streams hydrate the ravines and glens and the old farm ponds can be used as a doggie swimming pool if no one is around.

Trail Time
More than one hour.

"No one appreciates the very special genius of your conversation as a dog does."
-Christopher Morley

53
Wenonah Woods

The Park

Wenonah grew out of a resort community that was founded in 1872, carved from the surrounding Deptford area. It was later the location of a junior-high and high-school level military academy, until the late 1930s. Interconnected wooded trails loop around the southern half of the town from northwest to east.

The Walks

From the north, across from Wenonah Lake, the first trail is *Break Back Run*, winding along wooded stream valleys and ridges. Next is the *Clay Hill Trail* where the walking is level save for the namesake hill by a bend in the stream.

Burlington

Phone Number
- None

Website
- www.geocities.com/woodsofwenonah/html

Admission Fee
- None

Directions
- The town of Wenonah is on Route 553. The trails are accessed from several points around town including Hayes Road at East Mantua Avenue; the west end of West Cedar Street; and the east end of Pine Street.

The well-maintained *Glen Trail* connects the paths on both sides of the railroad. A brief side trail to Clinton Street leads to a tiny, stone fish pond, a quaint remnant of Wenonah's 19th century resort days. Continuing onto the *George Eldridge Trail*, the path features many streams and wooden bridges.

Side trails lead to more hiking on the *Deptford/Sewell Trails* and the *Monongahela Brook Trail*, a half-mile loop that rolls along the south shore and drops to a flat creekside return trip. Some of the biggest trees in the Wenonah Woods can be found here.

The last trail is *Covey's Lake Trail*, a 3/4-mile loop along the quiet tree-lined shore. The lake was once a center for leisurely recreation at the resort, sporting a boathouse and a teahouse. Watch for snakes in the rocks around the lake.

Trail Sense: The trails are not marked but wooden posts are prominently placed at trail junctions.

Dog Friendliness
Dogs are welcome along all the trails here.
Traffic
There are backyards every 15 minutes or so but not much competition on the trails.
Canine Swimming
At the northern terminus of Break Back Run Trail, across N. Jefferson Avenue is Davidson's Lake, a super canine swimming hole. Comey's Lake can be algae-encrusted but there is access to clear water near the wooden dock.
Trail Time
More than one hour.

54
Round Valley Recreation Area

The Park

A natural horseshoe-shaped basin enclosed on three sides by Cushetunk Mountain attracted the attention of the New Jersey Water Supply Association in the mid-1900s and the task of moving people and houses out of the deep, natural ravine and building two dams was completed by 1965. The reservoir has no natural drainage and is filled by pumping water up from the Raritan River. Since this is a costly proposition water is drawn from the 55-billion gallon reservoir only in emergencies. Thus the water level in Round Valley is consistently high, and the clarity exceptional.

Hunterdon

Phone Number
- None

Website
- www.state.nj.us/dep/parksand-forests/parks/round.html

Admission Fee
- Yes, from Memorial Day to Labor Day

Directions
- Take I-78 to Exit 18 (Route 22 East) and follow the signs to the park.

From the beginning Round Valley was created with recreation in mind. A campground was ready by 1972 and an earthen dam was constructed to form a swimming area. Today the park manages almost 4,000 acres, half of which are covered in water.

The Walks

Canine hiking in Round Valley is conducted on the *Cushetunk Trail,* a nine-mile natural surface path that leads to the wilderness camping sites. This is an out-and-back affair - you can not hike completely around the lake. Many canine hikers use a small beach about five miles in as a turning-around point.

Aside from the potential for many hours of trail time, the workout for your dog here is provided from some daunting ascents (and descents in the opposite direction). The trail dips in and out of wooded areas and views of the lake from different angles help inject variety into this trek.

You need not walk all day to make a trip to Round Valley with your dog worthwhile. The lake is a fantastic place to canoe with your dog or take him out on a fishing excursion - four record New Jersey fish have been plucked from these waters: a lake trout, a brown trout, a freshwater eel and a smallmouth bass.

Trail Sense: There are helpful signs at trail junctions and, more importantly, mile markers that allow you to determine when to turn around. The park will close on you if you don't return to your car in time.

Dog Friendliness
Dogs are allowed on the trails but not in the campground overnight.
Traffic
This is a popular summer destination and the trail is open to mountain bikes and horses.
Canine Swimming
The Cushetunk Trail touches down of the lake.
Trail Time
Open-ended, up to a full day.

55
Fort Mott State Park

The Park

Fort Mott was envisioned as part of a three-fort defense of Philadelphia that dangled across the Delaware River. Following the Civil War, work began on 11 gun emplacements but only two were completed when the fort was abandoned in 1876. In preparation for the Spanish-American War in 1896, Fort Mott, named to honor Major General Gershom Mott, a native of Bordentown, was completed and outfitted with three 10-inch and three 12-inch guns. The fort remained active until 1943, although during its last two decades the guns were dismantled and shipped elsewhere. In 1947 the State of New Jersey purchased Fort Mott as an historic site and opened the state park on June 24, 1951.

Salem

Phone Number
- (609) 935-3218

Website
- www.state.nj.us/dep/ forestry/parks/fortmot.htm

Admission Fee
- None

Directions
- From Exit 1 of I-295, take Route 49 East to Fort Mott Road. Turn right onto Fort Mott Road and travel three miles. The park is located on right.

The Walks

Fort Mott features a walking tour through the 19th-century defensive position that enables your dog to ramble through the gun batteries and ammunition magazines and to clamber on top of the massive protective parapet. This concrete wall was built of concrete poured 35 feet thick with an additional 60 feet of earth piled in front. Landscaping made the fort look like a big hill from the Delaware River.

In additon to this unique dog walk there is a groomed trail that winds through twelve-foot high swamp grasses to Finn's Point National Cemetery, the final resting place for 2,436 Confederate soldiers who perished in a Civil War prisoner of war camp at Fort Delaware.

Trail Sense: A map of the walking tour of is available.

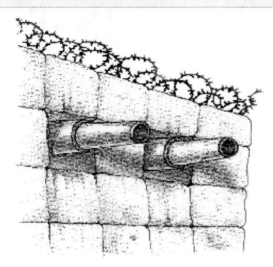

Dog Friendliness

Dogs are permitted in the state park.

Traffic

Not many people make their way to this remote outpost on the banks of the Delaware River.

Canine Swimming

Fort Mott State Park is the closest thing to an ocean swimming experience in the Delaware Valley. Below the ferry pier is a sand beach with enough wave action to convince your dog he's chasing that stick into the Atlantic.

Trail Time

About an hour, depending on how much time you spend on the beach.

Your dog will love the sandy beach and waves at Fort Mott State Park.

129

56
Forest Resource Education Center

The Park

The Forest Resource Education Center is exactly what it sounds like - a living outdoor classroom to teach New Jersey residents about trees. The State of New Jersey has 660 acres to demonstrate the practice of forest stewardship. In addition the New Jersey Forest Tree Nursery uses 45 acres for the propagation and production of more than 300,000 seedlings each year to supply community forestry programs throughout the state.

The Walks

Dogs are welcome to use the interpretive trails across the Education Center property. You may even be able to linger behind a passing class group and learn a few things about New Jersey forests. Several of the trail subjects are not your typical nature center fare: fire ecology and forest products, for instance.

There are a total of about five miles of formal trails and plenty of sand roads to wander around. This is all easy going for any dog, flat with paw-friendly surfaces. Of course there is plenty of shade on hot summer days.

Trail Sense: Trail guides are available in the center and there are information boards out by the trailheads.

Ocean

Phone Number
- (732) 928-2360

Website
- www.state.nj.us/dep/parksandforests/forest/njfs_frep.html

Admission Fee
- No

Directions
- From I-195 take Exit 21 (527/528 South) for 6.2 miles and turn right onto Bowman Blvd. After .9 miles turn right onto Don Connor Boulevard. The Interpretive Center is on the right.

"Properly trained, a man can be dog's best friend."
-Corey Ford

Dog Friendliness

Dogs are welcome to use the Education Center.

Traffic

If you come on a day without any group tours you may have the forest to yourself.

Canine Swimming

Small woodland ponds can provide sporadic refreshment.

Trail Time

More than one hour.

*Maple sugaring is just one of the things your dog can learn
about how to use the woods here.*

57

Garret Mountain Reservation

The Park

The Lenni Lenape Indians who once lived here used this mountain as a hunting grounds, chasing deer off the cliffs. Excitement on the mountain around the turn of the 20th century came in a quite different form - an amusement park.

In 1892 Catholina Lambert, one of the Silk Kings of Paterson - the Silk City - spent a half million dollars to build his Lambert Castle here from sandstone quarried on the mountain. Labor unrest led to financial difficulties for Lambert in 1914 and forced him to be mortgage his home. He died in 1923 at the age of 88 and several years later his son sold the castle to the City of Paterson for $125,000. Passaic County combined the Lambert estate with land purchased from the shuttered amusement park to create the 568-acre Garret Mountain Reservation.

Passaic

Phone Number
- (973) 881-4832

Website
- www.passaiccountynj.org/ ParksHistorical/Parks/garret- mountainreservation.htm

Admission Fee
- No

Directions
- From I-80 exit at Squirrel-wood/West Paterson (Exit 56 westbound, Exit 56A eastbound). On Squirrelwood Road continue through the traffic light and pass Berkeley College where the road becomes Rifle Camp Road. Make your first left onto Mountain Avenue and the park entrance on the right.

The Walks

The main canine hiking at Garret Mountain is found along a yellow-blazed path that loops the park for about three miles. The highlight of this circuit are the unobstructed views to the east from the edge of the ridge 500 feet above sea level. Paterson spreads out directly below and the Manhattan skyline is clearly visible in the distance. The Verrazzano-Narrows Bridge can even be seen on a bright day. There are no severe climbs to reach these spectacular vistas on this enjoyable hike with your dog.

Many folks shun the bridle paths and foot trails and use the winding park

park roads to hike with their dogs in the jogging/bike lanes.

Trail Sense: There is no park map although the lay of the land isn't hard to figure out. The trails have almost too many blazes and can be confusing at times.

Dog Friendliness
Dogs are everywhere at Garret Mountain.

Traffic
The park has an equestrian center and many visitors to share your outing with your dog.

Canine Swimming
Barbour's Pond is available for a doggie dip.

Trail Time
More than one hour.

Your dog can clearly see the Manhattan skyline from the trail at Garret Mountain.

58
Manasquan Reservoir

The Park

Manasquan Reservoir was completed in the late 1980s, the realization of a water supply plan to provide up to 30 million gallons of fresh water a day. Water is actually pumped through a five-foot diameter pipe for over five miles from the Manasquan River and stored in the 4-billion gallon capacity reservoir.

In 1990 Monmouth county entered into a 99-year agreement to manage recreation activities around the reservoir. Most of those activities take place on the 770 acres of water that dominate the 1,200-acre property.

Monmouth

Phone Number
- (732) 919-0096

Website
- www.monmouthcountyparks.com/parks/manasquan_park.asp

Admission Fee
- None

Directions
- From I-195 take Exit 28 onto Route 9, heading north. Make a right onto Georgia Tavern Road and another right on Windeler Road to the Visitor Center.

The Walks

In a state of few natural lakes, this is one of the longest walks you can take with your dog around water in New Jersey. The canine hiking here is performed mostly on a gray, crushed-gravel multi-use path that circumnavigates the reservoir for five miles. Of course, once you sign on for this journey you are in for all five miles. If you do want to just walk out and turn around, concentrate your explorations to the southwestern section of the trail. There are three access points to the perimeter trail, all in this area.

There is a good deal of diversity despite the confined spaces of the trail. You will take your dog through wetlands and grassy plains and airy woodlands. Of course you will get your share of long views across open water. The terrain is mostly level throughout to promote a pleasant pace.

Trail Sense: There is a trailmap available that you can refer to not so much for wayfinding as to mark your progress around the reservoir.

More than 200 species of birds have found their way to this relatively new body of water, including bald eagles. Manasquan Reservoir is the best site to view bald eagles in Monmouth County. Bald eagles mate for life and a nesting pair has taken residence in the western area of the park. During the early summer, baby eagles can be seen near the nest practicing their flying and hunting abilities as they mimic their parents.

Dog Friendliness
Dogs are permitted on the park's trails.
Traffic
The perimeter trail is popular with joggers, cyclists and even horses.
Canine Swimming
Most of the time you are traveling above the water line.
Trail Time
Allow two hours to complete the trip around Manasquan Reservoir..

59
Turkey Swamp Park

The Park

The first human habitation of this land was by the Lenni Lenape, an Algonquian group of Indians who lived in loosely-knit family groups in the greater Delaware area. The tribe camped along the Metedeconk River and excavations are ongoing to learn more about their life here.

Turkey Swamp Park is a combination woodland park and family campground. Don't come looking for turkeys - the park is named for the village of Turkey, now called Adelphia.

The Walks

There are two distinct options for canine hikers at Turkey Swamp. The *Old Lenape Trail* skips off through the pitch pine and blueberry bush landscape common in the northern reaches of the Pine Barrens. The sandy soil is easy on the paws - too easy in wet times as the trail turns swampy.

Monmouth

Phone Number
- (732) 462-7286

Website
- www.monmouthcountyparks.com/parks/turkey.asp

Admission Fee
- None

Directions
- From the New Jersey Turnpike take Exit 7A and head east on I-195. Take Exit 22. Turn left and go north on Jackson Mills Road. Turn left at the light for Georgia Road and continue to park/campground entrance on the left.

In the other direction is the orange-blazed *Alder Trail* that circles a 17-acre man-made lake. The route links picnic areas and provides several access points to superb dog paddling, especially when the campground is closed. This is also an easy hike for your dog, alternating between open fields and light woods.

The *Metedeconk Trail* takes your dog trhough a pitch pine lowland forest on natural surfaces and boardwalks. Along the way, look for tiny "volcanoes" that are actually ant nests.

Trail Sense: The trails are well-blazed and a map is available at the campground office. If you lose the blazes around the lake just keep hugging the shoreline until the route reappears.

Dog Friendliness

Dogs are permitted on the trails *and* allowed in the campground - this is a county park, not a state park.

Traffic

In the off-season you may have the trails to yourself; when the campground is open you will be dodging mountain bikes and horses on the multi-use trails.

Canine Swimming

In the lake when there are no fishermen, this is an excellent dog swimming pool.

Trail Time

About one hour.

The easy access to the lake at Turkey Swamp makes it especially appealing to canine swimmers.

60
Hedden County Park

The Park

The local Hedden family of Dover donated the original 40 acres for this park in 1963. Over the years Morris County has increased the size of Hedden Park to 380 acres west of Dover.

There are two distinct sections: the pond section with a fishing pier, boathouse and outdoor fireplace for ice skaters and the Concord Road section with an open playing field and a forested hiking area.

The Walks

This is an unexpected canine hiking paradise in a residential setting. From the Concord Road lot you can jump in the middle of the feature trail in the park, the white-blazed *Hedden Circular Trail*. From a rather benign beginning this surprisingly sporty two-mile loop gets interesting in a hurry as you and your dog work along the curves of a rocky hillside. The truly adventurous dog will want to cut the loop short and try the red-blazed *Mountain Trail*. It picks its way straight up the slope. The paths are studded with rocks but of the worn-down, smaller variety - not the monstrous boulders of some neighboring parks.

For more relaxed canine hiking take your dog along the *Indian Falls Trail* and the *Jackson Brook Trail* that trace the lively stream through a shady glen. These two are both out-and-back affairs but well worth retracing your pawprints. Indian Falls is Hedden Park's best-known attraction.

Trail Sense: A detailed trail map is available and the trails are reliably blazed.

Morris

Phone Number
- None

Website
- www.morrisparks.net/parks/heddenmain.htm

Admission Fee
- No

Directions
- The park adjoins the town of Dover. From Route 10 take Dover-Chester Road north to a T-interesection. Make a left and a right on Concord Road and follow into the park or make a right on Reservoir Avenue and left on Hawthorne Street into the park.

Your dog will walk on plenty of rocks in Hedden County Park - both on the trail and through streams.

Dog Friendliness

Dogs are allowed throughout the park.

Traffic

You won't have any problem finding solitude in Hedden Park on the Hedden Circular Trail.

Canine Swimming

Jackson Brook provides a refreshing respite and a small six-acre pond is at the end of the Indian Falls Trail.

Trail Time

More than one hour.

61
Mount Hope Historical Park

The Park

The first iron ore was pulled from the ground in this area almost 300 years ago. There were three plump veins or ore, known as the Brennan, Mount Pleasant, and Richard veins. John Jacob Fresch, a Swiss immigrant, built the Mount Hope Furnace in 1772 and the forge was kept busy during the Revolutionary War producing shot, shells and cannon for the Continental Army.

The park is on the site of three of the most productive mines in the state. The furnace fired for the last time in 1825 but high grade magnetite iron ore was mined here from the early 1800s to 1978.

Morris

Phone Number
- None

Website
- www.morrisparks.org/parks/mhmain.htm

Admission Fee
- None

Directions
- Exit into Dover from I-80 at Exit 35B and turn right onto Mt. Hope Avenue. Turn onto Richard Mine Road to Teabo Road and the park.

The Walks

From an unpromising start up a rock road and under utility wires this turns into a fine ramble through the remnants of some of the score of 18th century iron mines that once operated in Mount Hope. Working on a wide, somewhat rocky trail you will twist past old building foundations and yawning open pits that nature is rapidly taking back from almost three centuries of mining activity.

There are several trails through the airy woods but you will want to use the *Red Trail* first. After a short tail this walking path takes in most of the mining relics at Mount Hope as it moves down a hillside in a counterclockwise loop for 1.5 miles. This trail is joined by another moderate-length loop, the *Orange Trail*, that will expand your dog's time at Mount Hope to over an hour. At the trail junction if you are looking to stay on the Red Trail bear left at the bottom of the hill since the red and orange blazes look identical in bright sunlight.

The *Blue Trail*, short but steep, goes to the Old Teabo mine and the *White Trail*, another quick one, goes to the Brennan mine. All told there are about four miles of quiet trails through this once-bustling series of hills.

Trail Sense: The trails are well-blazed and signed and if you are lucky there may be maps left at the trailhead.

Dog Friendliness
Dogs are welcome to enjoy this view into New Jersey's mining past.
Traffic
Expect little, if any.
Canine Swimming
None.
Trail Time
About one hour.

62
Eno's Pond County Park

The Park

With the advent of the tourism in the late1800s Lacey became a summer destination for the wealthy. Several large hotel resorts sprang up in the township. In 1889 Byron E. Eno purchased the Riverside House and built a dam to enlarge the Colonial-era pond adjacent to his hotel. He used the pond to harvest ice in the winter to store for his summer guests.

By the 1940s beach houses were replacing seasonal hotels and the Riverside House declined until it was finally destroyed by a fire in 1952. Eno's ice pond remains and has become the centerpiece for a county park along the south shore of Bridge Creek. The casino that was part of Eno's resort still stands and operates as the Captain's Inn.

Ocean

Phone Number
- (877) 627-2757

Website
- http://www.ocean.nj.us/parks/enos.html

Admission Fee
- None

Directions
- Take Exit 74 off the Garden State Parkway, going east on Lacey Road. Cross over Route 9 onto East Lacey Road for another mile and the park entrance on the left past the Captains Inn.

The Walks

Eno's Pond County Park abuts the Forsythe National Wildlife Refuge and the two have joined forces to create a trail system through a regenerative forest. One of the two trails is handicapped-accessible and canine hikers will want to concentrate on the other - the *Nature Trail* that swallows much of its fellow trail anyway.

This is an exceedingly pleasant 1.1-mile hike with your dog, enhanced by one of the better trail guides to be found in New Jersey parks. This is easy-going on a variety of surfaces completely in a shaded loop.

Trail Sense: The trails are well-marked with signage and numbered stops on the Nature Trail. A map is found in the centerfold of the trail guides and a mapboard can be consulted at the trailhead.

Dog Friendliness

Dogs are welcome on these trails and poop bags are available at the parking lot.

Traffic

Foot traffic only on the Nature Trail and it thins out away from the picnic area.

Canine Swimming

Your dog can slip into Eno's Pond for some refreshing dog-paddling.

Trail Time

Less than one hour.

*It is easy going for dogs through the diverse
maritime forest at Eno's Pond.*

63
Voorhees State Park

The Park

Former New Jersey governor Foster M. Voorhees donated his 325-acre Hill Acres estate to the state for a park in 1925. The honorable Governor Voorhees died in 1927 and in another decade he wouldn't recognize his old farm.

Beginning in 1933 a Civilian Conservation Corps unit of 200 men set up camp in Voorhees State Park, working here and in Hacklebarney State Park cutting trails, building stone picnic shelters, carving roads and planting thousands of trees.

Today Voorhees State Park is over 1,000 wooded acres. It is a recreation center for campers, picnickers and ballplayers.

Hunterdon

Phone Number
- (908) 638-6969

Website
- http://www.state.nj.us/dep/parksandforests/parks/voorhees.html

Admission Fee
- None

Directions
- From I-78 take Route 31 North. Turn right on Route 513 North. After passing through the town of High Bridge, the park entrance will be on the left.

The Walks

The trail system at Voorhees is built around seven out-and-back trails that can be cobbled together to form canine hiking loops such as the orange-blazed *Brookside Trail* and the green-blazed *Tanglewood Trail* around the main drive with the Blue Trail to form a 5.3-mile loop. Two of the premier paths at Voorhees link the two main segments of the park: the blue-blazed *Hill Acres Trail* leads to a scenic view through a cut in the trees and the *Cross Park Trail*, the sole footpath-only trail here, leads to the astronomical observatory.

Most of the paths in Voorhees are multi-use; not paved but often gravelly under paw. Some dog walkers just use the main paved road that loops through the park. Voorhees radiates an aura of leisurely strolling on its wide paths but vigorous canine hikers can find some challenges on the wooded slopes as well.

Trail Sense: There are maps, signs at the trailheads and blazes on the trails. No excuse to lose your way here.

Dog Friendliness

Dogs are welcome in Voorhees State park but cannot stay overnight in the campgrounds.

Traffic

You should be able to find stretches of trail to enjoy with your dog alone. Most of the trails host bikes as well.

Canine Swimming

There is a pond on the property but this isn't a prime destination for water-loving dogs.

Trail Time

A couple hours or more is possible.

64
Swartswood State Park

The Park

This is New Jersey's first state park. The entire state park system grew from a 12.5-acre gift from George M. Emmans, made with "an inent that people may have use of the premises herein conveyed as a public park forever." New Jersey's first ever state park land is now the Emmans Grove Picnic Area.

Swartswood Lake was scraped out by a retreating glacier 15,000 years ago and the 700 acres of glittering water remains the star of the park. The name derives from Captain Anthony Swartwout, whose farm was overrun by Delaware Indians and some white settlers dressed as Indians in the French and Indian War in 1755. His wife and three children were caught outside and killed, leaving Captain Swartwout and three more children to surrender. About a mile from the cabin Swartwout was tortured, disemboweled and left to die.

Sussex

Phone Number
- (973) 383-5230

Website
- www.state.nj.us/dep/park-sandforests/parks/swartswood.html

Admission Fee
- Yes, during summer in the recreation area

Directions
- From I-80, take Exit 25, Route 206 north to Newton, about 12 miles. From Newton, make a left at the second traffic light (Route 206 and Spring Street) then make a left at the next light onto Route 519. Follow 519 for approximately 1/2 mile, then make a left onto Route 622 at Sussex County College sign. Follow Route 622 for about 4 1/2 miles. Turn left onto Route 619. The park entrance is about 1/2 mile south on Route 619.

The Walks

There are two hiking options for canine hikers in Swartswood State Park. Across from the park entrance is a multi-use trail system consisting of *Duck Pond Trail* (paved for its half-mile length) and leading to the 2.8-mile *Spring Lake Trail*. Dogs are rewarded for completing this hilly loop with a dip in the secluded Spring Lake. Most dogs probably won't take note of the impressive old growth hemlock stands along the way. Be aware that this area is open to hunting in season.

A better first choice would be the *Grist Mill Trail* in the isolated western section of the park. This hearty 40-minute loop uses switchbacks to advance on a cedar forest on the upper slopes. Feel free to stop frequently so your dog can catch his breath and you can enjoy long views of Swartswood Lake. The trail is well-maintained and open to foot traffic only.

Trail Sense: A park map and trail map are available and the routes are well-marked.

Dog Friendliness
Dogs are allowed to use these trails and can go anywhere no one is swimming. Dogs are not permitted in the campground.

Traffic
Most people consider this Swartswood Lake and not Swartswood State Park so when you head off on the trails you will be leaving most visitors behind.

Canine Swimming
Of course - but even better than you may think. At the boat ramp for Little Swartswood Lake and the boat ramp at Snake Island on the westen shores of Swartswood Lake both have piers that are ideal for a little dock diving practice.

Trail Time
More than one hour.

The swimming is easy for dogs in Swartswood Lake.

65
Herrontown Woods

The Park

Herrontown Woods was the former home of Oswald Veblen, an Iowa-born mathematician whose work in geometry at Princeton University was internationally acclaimed. Veblen spent many an hour in his private sanctuary and probably blazed some of the the park's trails. The top academic prize in geometry awarded each year is named for Oswald Veblen, who deeded this land to Mercer County in 1957.

In the 1970s the county acquired additional property to bring the park to its current size of 142 acres.

Mercer
Phone Number - None
Website - http://www.princetontwp.org/herron.html
Admission Fee - None
Directions - Take Route 27 (Nassau Street) from the center of Princeton to Snowden Lane. Make a left and follow Snowden to the parking lot.

The Walks

Your dog will be completely surrounded by the smells of eastern deciduous forest in Herrontown Woods. Oak, gum, tulip and red maple are the dominant trees here. Start with a tour of the property on an outer ring that rises about 150 feet in elevation. The trails alternate between paw-friendly dirt (the soft paths can be muddy through wetland areas) and rockier ground. Watch for rooty spots.

Once you have completed the outer loop you can continue your canine hike on the various inner trails. All told there are about three miles of woody paths here.

Trail Sense: There is a detailed, but fading topographic map at the parking lot. Color blazes are faded and a small wooden stake with a painted crown pops up occasionally. In other words, come to Herrontown Woods with a mind to explore the boundary fences and private property signs will keep you corralled.

As you hike with your dog through Herrontown Woods
keep a look out for quarry holes.
The diabase, or traprock, formed when molten magma
pushed its way through cracks in the surface.
Among the many uses for the hard stone
is roadbuilding.

Dog Friendliness
Dogs are allowed in the Herrontown Woods.
Traffic
This is a quiet park, reserved for hikers.
Canine Swimming
Seasonal streams provide little more than a splash or two.
Trail Time
An hour or more is possible.

66
Hunterdon County Arboretum

The Park

George Bloomer opened a commercial nursery on this location in 1953. The core of his business was the spruces and hardwoods commonly known to backyards throughout New Jersey but he also grew exotic trees like Amur cork trees from Manchuria and dawn redwoods, an ancient tree known only through fossils until 1941 when a botany student tracked down living specimens in rural China.

Bloomer's wife Esther founded the Hunderdon County SPCA in 1965. He sold his 73-acre site to the county in 1974 to be used for public education.

Hunterdon

Phone Number
- (973) 875-4800

Website
- http://www.co.hunterdon.
nj.us/depts/parks/guides/
Arbortum.htm

Admission Fee
- None

Directions
- The Arboretum is 5 miles north of Flemington on the east side of Route 31.

Across the road behind the Arboretum are 32 additional acres that were once the property of J.C. Furnas, writer, historian and biographer. His most famous work was a case for safe driving, published in Reader's Digest in August 1935. It became perhaps the most widely circulated article ever written with eight million reprint copies distributed. Furnas left the land to the county after his death in 2001 at the age of 95. It is currently undeveloped.

The Walks

Dogs are often banned from arboretums so it is a treat to be able to enjoy this living tree museum with your dog. There are two miles of easy canine hiking on wide and flat dirt trails that are broken into small segments. In addition to the wide variety of trees and shrubs there are display gardens of native and non-native flowers.

A good way to approach the Arboretum is to take your dog on a circuit of the 1.1-mile *Outer Loop Trail* that visits tree plantations and wetlands. With this overview you can then re-visit some of the short connecting trails.

Trail Sense: A park map and signs lead you around the Arboretum.

Dog Friendliness

Dogs are allowed on the Arboretum trails.

Traffic

The quiet trails are for foot traffic only.

Canine Swimming

The pond and stream across the property are not for canine aquatics.

Trail Time

About one hour to see all the trails.

"Children are for people who can't have dogs."
-Anonymous

67

John A. Roebling Park

The Park

John Augustus Roebling was born in Prussia in 1806 and came to Pittsburgh at the age of 25. Although a trained engineer, he and his brother came to America to farm. His agrarian pursuits were none too successful and he began doing engineering work for the state of Pennsylvania when he hit upon the idea of twisted metal wire to suspend long bridge spans.

Roebling completed his first suspension bridge in 1845 and became succesful enough to expand his business. He purchased 25 acres in Trenton for his wire factory in 1850.

Roebling won the contract to build the Brooklyn Bridge but suffered

Mercer
Phone Number - None
Website - http://www.mercercounty.org/parks/parks.htm
Admission Fee - None
Directions - From Route 206 (South Broad Street), turn onto West Park Avenue. Make a left turn onto Wescott Avenue. After passing under high tension wires, make an immediate right turn onto the lane that leads to the park.

an injury early during the construction. He never recovered and died in 1869. His son Washington completed the masterwork and the family business continued to expand. The land for the John A. Roebling Park was donated by the family in the 1950s.

The Walks

When the first sign a dog owner sees upon entering a park is NO DUMPING it is a good indication there aren't likely to be many prohibitions against dogs. Such is the case at John A. Roebling Park.

There are two disparite trail systems in the park. The *Watson Woods Trail* and the *Abbott Brook Trail* move through some scruffy, wooded wetlands. Your dog may have to pick his way through some blowdowns and overgrown vines on these barely maintained paths. A dirt road can be used for elbow room and to complete a canine loop hike.

In the opposite direction is open walking into the marshes on the *Spring Lake Trail*. Don't be put off by the trash, old tires and power lines as you hike past Rowan Lake. Things improve as you shortly reach Spring Lake and get better still as you circle the lake and cross into the North Marsh.

The trail system on the small marsh island is quite elaborate, with plenty to see. The highlight are the beaver lodges and turtles can often be seen soaking in the sun on a bright summer day. This is easy canine hiking, if in an industrial setting.

Trail Sense: There is no map at the park but there are enough signs and blazes to keep your interest.

Dog Friendliness
Dogs are welcome in John A. Roebling Park.

Traffic
This is not the first choice for many people looking for an outdoor adventure.

Canine Swimming
There are places where your dog can slip into the open water of Spring Lake for canine aquatics.

Trail Time
A leisurely hour.

"Money will buy a pretty good dog but it won't buy the wag of his tail."
-Josh Billings

68
Rancocas State Park

The Park

The main branch of the Rancocas Creek, the largest watershed in south-central New Jersey, fractures into tributaries at this spot. The major tribes of the Lenni Lenape found their way to the Rancocas, probably named for one of the sub-tribes, sometime after the 1400s.

European settlement - and diseases - eventually displaced the Lenni Lenape. In the late 19th century members of the Powhatan Renape Nation, descended from the Nanticoke of southern Delaware and the Rappahannocks of Virginia, began trickling into a tiny hamlet known as Morrisville to establish a community.

Burlington

Phone Number
- (609) 726-1191

Website
- http://www.nj.gov/dep/park-sandforests/parks/rancocas.html

Admission Fee
- None

Directions
- From the Mount Holly Bypass go west on Marne Highway (Route 537) and make first right on Deacon Road to end after 1.3 miles.

As a state park, Rancocas is so underfunded that it once had to close for several years in the 1970s. It's a park again but still far from robust. The New Jersey Audubon Society leases part of the park's 1,252 acres to help it survive.

The Walks

Active dog owners are a lot that can appreciate a shabby park. The lack of visitation is typically accompanied by a similar lack of restrictions against dogs. When you arrive at Rancocas don't expect to be greeted by any typical state park amenities such as entrance signs, visitor centers or trail maps. Just perfect for a dog ready to explore.

And there is plenty to escape to at Rancocas. A tangle of unmarked paths and sand roads provide access to freshwater tidal creeks, dark forests, open meadows, and reedy marshes. Expect to encounter an overgrown patch here and there - a small price to pay for the uncrowded trails.

The canine hiking here is mostly flat along paw-friendly soft dirt and sand. A complete tour of the peninsular property will push you out near the confluence of the North and South branches of the Rancocas Creek with wide-angle views of the aquatic merger.

Trail Sense: There are no navigational aids available but the short, interconnecting roads should give you confidence to push further into Rancocas.

Dog Friendliness
Dogs can run on most of the property but are not allowed on the trails of the Rancocas Nature Center.

Traffic
Dirt bikes and the occasional vehicle on the sand roads are normally a minor concern.

Canine Swimming
Fishermen's trails often lead from the sand roads along the waterways and offer good swimming opportunities in the Rancocas Creek branches.

Trail Time
Several hours to circle the peninsula are possible.

"They are superior to human beings as companions.
They do not quarrel or argue with you.
They never talk about themselves but listen to you while you
talk about yourself, and keep an appearance of being interested
in the conversation."

-Jerome K. Jerome

69
Mercer Lake County Park

The Park

This is the flagship of the Mercer County park system with about 2,500 acres. Just about any recreation idea you can come up with will be satisfied here: a dozen ballfields, top-notch tennis courts, miles of biked paths and, out on Lake Mercer, world class sculling.

The Walks

Most of the hikable trails at Mercer County Park are south of the lake. The main paved trail that hugs the shoreline on a peninsula to the left of the marina is one choice for canine hikers. Another is the mountain bike trail system that runs for miles through the wooded areas around the lake. There are some ups and downs but apparently not enough to make this a biking hotbed so you may be able to find some relaxing canine hiking here.

North of the lake, across the power line, is dominated by the *Blue Trail*. The trail system is not as elaborate on the north side and once you sign on to the Blue Trail you will have to take it the whole way.

Perhaps the best route for canine hikers in Mercer County Park is one of your own design. There are plenty of islands of greenspace that alternate with stands of trees and you can take your dog on your own adventure.

Trail Sense: There is a park mapboard but no trail map and don't be surprised if you wander down a path that takes you off the property or just ends.

Dog Friendliness

Dogs are welcome in the non-recreational areas of Mercer County Park.

Traffic

The park gets plenty of use from tennis players, rowers, cyclists, picnickers,
ballplayers and more but it is possible to find some private space for you and
your dog if you need it.

Canine Swimming

There are plenty of places for a doggie swim in Lake Mercer.

Trail Time

Anywhere from a quick romp in the dog park to a half-day of walking.

70
Taylor Wildlife Preserve

The Park

In 1720 Joshua Wright purchased land along the Delaware River known to the local Indians as "the island" since it often remained dry during the periodic flooding of the river, which rises and falls as much as five feet between high and low tides. The land has remained in his family ever since. In 1975 Sylvia and Joshua Taylor donated 89 acres of their 130-acre property to the New Jersey National Lands Trust and opened the Taylor Wildlife Preserve to the public.

Burlington

Phone Number
- None

Website
- None

Admission Fee
- None

Directions
- Taylor Wildlife Preserve is east of Riverton, off River Road (Route 543). The main entrance is on Taylors Lane and the trails can also be accessed from Inman Street.

The Walks

One of the few remaining accessible open spaces remaining along the heavily industrialized Delaware River is at Taylor Wildlife Preserve. As it is, the preserve is squeezed against the water by four neighboring industrial parks. A 12-step interpretive trail has been carved around a vibrant freshwater marsh. For the most part the trails are dirt and stony. Several benches have been provided overlooking the marsh and the Delaware River. The walk along the river is one of the longest in the area and dogs can easily reach the water for a swim.

Trail Sense: Grassy areas can become overgrown and yellow-backed directional markers have been strategically placed.

Dog Friendliness
Dogs are welcome in the wildlife preserve.
Traffic
There are no horses or bikes to dodge here.
Canine Swimming
There is easy access to the Delaware River for good dog paddling.
Trail Time
Less than an hour.

*"Ever consider what they must think of us? I mean,
here we come back from the grocery store with the most
amazing haul - chicken, pork, half a cow...
They must think we're the greatest hunters on earth!"*
-Anne Tyler

71
Crow's Woods

The Park

The area was first settled in 1682 but things didn't really get going until 21-year old Elizabeth Haddon arrived in 1701 to establish her father's claims here. It wasn't until 1875 that Haddonfield Borough was officially established and the natural area south of town has been known as Crow's Woods for nearly as long.

For years part of the area was used as a landfill which was converted into playing fields following the 1967 construction of the PATCO Hi-Speed Line which abuts the park. Today, the grounds at Crow's Woods encompass more than 65 acres.

Burlington
Phone Number - None
Website - None
Admission Fee - None
Directions - From King's Highway West head towards the Hi-Speed Line overpass and make a left on Warwick Road. After one mile make a left onto Upland Way and make a right just past the underpass into the park. Follow the park road to the end.

The Walks

Crow's Woods packs plenty of topographical diversity into its short, intermingling trails. In fact, so many dog walkers have come from outside Haddonfield to enjoy the park's ravines and hills that borough commissioners have considered imposing a "use tag" system similar to New Jersey beaches.

The wide, soft dirt paths wind through dense woodlands of scrub oak, pitch pine and mountain laurel. An asphalt jogging track around the perimeter of the sports fields is also available.

Trail Sense: Three trails are blazed in blue, yellow and white but any route can be improvised in the compact Crow's Woods without fear of becoming lost.

Dog Friendliness

Dogs are permitted off leash in the woods but must be restrained near the playing fields.

Traffic

In addition to dog walkers, Crow's Woods is popular with mountain bikers.

Canine Swimming

There are small swimming holes in the woods that are more suited for a refreshing splash than sustained dog paddling.

Trail Time

Less than an hour.

"If you don't think dogs can count, try putting three dog biscuits in your pocket and giving Fido two."
-Phil Pastoret

72

Cape May National Wildlife Refuge

The Park

The Cape May National Wildlife Refuge became one of the newest refuges in the federal system when a modest 90 acres were acquired in 1989. The vision for the refuge calls for 21,200 acres to be brought under protection in this key location along the Atlantic Flyway. The U.S. Fish and Wildlife Service is about half way to realizing that goal.

Included in its more than 11,000 acres is a five-mile stretch along the Delaware Bay. Faced with 12 miles of open water to cross during their seasonal migration songbirds and raptors spend extra time on Cape May Point resting and feeding. So many shorebirds linger here during migration that it is second only to Copper River Delta in Alaska as a shorebird staging area.

Cape May

Phone Number
- (609) 463-0994

Website
- http://www.fws.gov/northeast/capemay/

Admission Fee
- None

Directions
- The Headquarters Office is west of Cape May Court House on Kimbles Beach Road, directly off Route 47.

The Walks

Cape May National Wildlife Refuge is divided into three divisions. The Cedar Swamp Division has no maintained trails and the Two-Mile Unit does not allow dogs so canine hikers will want to head to the Delaware Bay Division at the Headquarters.

There is a short, winding crushed gravel trail at the Headquarters but dog owners will start here only to pick up a trail map. The prime destination is the next road south at Woodcock Lane. The *Woodcock Trail* is a one-mile stacked loop trail that skirts a woodland habitat. The mown grass path is wide enough to keep your dog centered and out of the reach of hitchhiking ticks in the tall grasses.

Spur trails jut into the surrounding woodlands and fingers of trail reach into the expansive salt marsh at the edge of the Delaware Bay. All the canine hiking in the national refuge is easy and flat.

Trail Sense: Signposts point you down the trails here and a park map is available.

Dog Friendliness
Dogs can hike the trails in the Delaware Bay Division but are banned from using the Two-Mile Unit.

Traffic
Bikes and horses are not permitted to use the refuge trails. The parking lot on Woodcock Lane can handle about a half-dozen vehicles so don't look for much competition for these trails.

Canine Swimming
There are no swimming opportunities here for your dog.

Trail Time
The main Woodcock loop and its spurs can be completed in about one hour. What's the hurry? Do the loop again.

The refuge trails lead out into the great marsh on the Delaware River.

73
Ocean County Park

The Park

In 1879 a New York banker named Charles Henry Kimball stopped in town to stay with a friend. During his visit he noticed his weak lungs flourished in the pine-studded community. He decided to move to the area and develop a resort that soon was attracting socially prominent visitors, many who decided to stay.

One who returned to live was John D. Rockefeller who built a 610-acre estate on Ocean Avenue. After his death in 1937 his son John, Jr., who would donate $537 million (in World War II money) over his lifetime, gave his father's summer playground to Ocean County for its first park in 1940.

Ocean
Phone Number - (877) 921-0074
Website - http://www.co.ocean.nj.us/parks/ocp.html
Admission Fee - None
Directions - The park is east of Lakewood on Ocean Avenue (Route 88) between Route 9 and the Garden State Parkway.

The park has played host to a variety of recreational pursuits, including a stint as spring training home to the New York baseball Giants. Today the park's 323 acres attracts fishermen, picnickers, tennis players, softball players, swimmers, cyclists and more.

The Walks

A phalanx of majestic silver-green pine trees immediately separate Ocean County park from the hub-bub of its surroundings. You can hike with your dog around the former Rockefeller grounds on the main paved park roadway or by dirt paths around the perimeter.

Regular visitors can take advantage of a fee-supported dog park that covers five acres in the back of the park. There is a gated, fenced-in area mostly for small dogs and an off-leash open field and wooded area for more spirited romps. If walking your dog around the main road look for a small cemetery for dogs that have served Ocean County, located just before the roadway to the dog park.

Trail Sense: A park map is available but you can go without it.

164

Dog Friendliness
Dogs are not allowed in the beach area of the swimming pond.
Traffic
Ocean County Park is a busy place but you can steer your dog to a quiet corner if you so desire.
Canine Swimming
When it is not crowded you dog can jump in Lake Fishigan for a refreshing swim.
Trail Time
About one hour.

74
Poricy Park

The Park

Poricy Park is a nature preserve
owned by Middletown Township. The
250-acre park includes woodlands,
fields, stream and marsh ecosystems,
and a bed of Cretaceous fossils, known
to collectors throughout the Northeast.

Joseph Murray farmed this land
in Colonial times. In 1780 Murray, a
member of the Monmouth Militia,
was shot down by British loyalists in his
cornfield in what is now Poricy Park's
New Jersey State Historic Site. The
Murray Farmhouse in the park dates to
1777.

The farm remained in the Murray
family until 1861 and was farmed continuously thereafter. In 1969 a plan to
reroute a sewer line through the brook triggered a citizen outrage that saved
these 250 acres from further development.

Monmouth

Phone Number
- (732) 842-5966

Website
- www.monmouth.com/
~poricypark/index.html

Admission Fee
- No

Directions
- The Nature Center is located
on Oak Hill Road in Middletown, just west of Route 35.
There are directional signs
posted on Route 35 and the
Parkway exits.

The Walks

There is a nice mix of open field and light woods canine hiking across the
wedge of land the makes up Poricy Park. The fields are paw-friendly mown grass
that support a meadow habitat. There are many short, intersecting trails cut into
the grassland maze that suggest extra time should be devoted to exploration with
your dog. This is all easy canine hiking.

Other spots to visit include Sassafras and Nut Grove with nut-bearing trees,
a natural marsh area that is about 10 degrees warmer in winter than other areas
in the park and a butterfly garden planted outside the Nature Center. The garden
features a variety of feeders.

Trail Sense: A trail map is available.

Dog Friendliness
Dogs are permitted in Poricy Park.

Traffic
Foot traffic only.

Canine Swimming
There is a pond at the base of a small cliff that you can make your way down to; but be careful of its muddy shore.

Trail Time
Less than one hour.

"Dogs' lives are too short. Their only fault, really."
-Agnes Sligh Turnbull

75
Cooper River Park

The Park

People began settling along the Cooper and Newton creeks in the 1690s as the waterways became busy conduits for goods to and from a young Philadelphia. Through the decades the free flow of water became strangled by all manner of debris and waste tumbling from the industrializing banks. In 1936 workers from the Works Project Administration waded into the putrid Cooper River swamp to build a dam, shove around mountains of dirt and shaped the creek into the slender lake that is the centerpiece of Cooper River Park.

Camden

Phone Number
- None

Website
- None

Admission Fee
- None

Directions
- Cooper River Park is in Pennsauken, traversed by Park Drive North and Park Drive South. Access is from Cuthbert Boulevard to the east and Crescent Boulevard (Route 130) to the west.

The Walks

A 3.8-mile paved pathway loops around the active lake. The serpentine route features almost continually unobstructed views of the water, which on most days will be sprinkled with sailors from the Cooper River Yacht Club on the south shore. Long stretches of the walk, especially in the eastern end of the park, are bereft of recreational activity, leaving you alone with other dog walkers and joggers. A number of war memorial monuments and statues grace the route.

Trail Sense: There is no map available but the park boundaries are only several yards from the lake on both sides.

Dog Friendliness

At the far eastern shore of the lake, at the terminus of North Shore Drive is a designated Pooch Park with two small enclosed dog runs, one for dogs over 30 pounds and another for smaller dogs. The lighted facility is open every day from 6 a.m. to 10 p.m., although the lights are more ornamental than functional.

Traffic

Cooper River is a busy urban park and expect any manner of use of these pathways.

Canine Swimming

There is access to the water at many points along the paved trail.

Trail Time

Less than one hour.

76
Teetertown Ravine Nature Preserve
Hunterdon County

From I-78 proceed north on Route 31 for 1.7 miles to Route 513 North. Turn right through High Bridge toward Califon for about 6.5 miles. Just past the A&P, turn left onto Sliker Road. Turn right onto Teetertown Road. Follow the left fork of the road about 1 mile to the stop sign at Hollow Brook Road. Turn left and proceed 0.1 mile up the ravine. There are vehicle pull-offs near the trailheads.

German immigrant John Teeter purchased a mill here in 1814, giving his name to the town the mill supported. His house still stands and 150 years later Merv Griffin lived in it. The Teetertown Ravine Nature Preserve was created to keep this lush valley in a natural state and additional sections have been acquired since 1999 to bring the total preserve to 682 acres.

A plethora of shortish trails provide great variety in open fields and diverse woodlands. An old farm serves up ponds and an old peach orchard. Be prepared for some steep hilly areas - your reward being a pleasing view of the valley.

Hunting is allowed in the preserve so save your visit to Teetertown Ravine for a Sunday during hunting season.

77
Farny State Park
Morris County

Take I-80 West to Exit 37 (Hibernia/Rockaway). At the bottom of the ramp, turn left onto Green Pond Road (County 513). Follow Green Pond Road north through the town and turn right onto Upper Hibernia Road (opposite the Marcella Community Center). After a mile turn left go 1.2 miles to a large dirt parking area on the left side of the road, just after crossing the dam of the Split Rock Reservoir.

Farny State Park, despite its location in the center of North Jersey, is one of the least-used parks in the state. There are no spectacular must-see destinations and the canine hiking is quite rugged with plenty of climbs and stream crossings that can be tricky when waters run high.

Much of your day here will be on the blue-blazed *Split Rock Loop Trail* and the *Four Birds Trail*, named for North American wild turkeys in the deciduous forests, red-tailed hawks above the cliffs, osprey along the lake shores, and great blue heron in the beaver meadows. Look for remnants of mining that once took place around Split Rock Reservoir as you work these trails.

78
Eagle Rock Reservoir
Essex County

Take I-280 East to Exit 8B (Prospect Avenue/Cedar Grove) onto Prospect Avenue in West Orange. Turn right onto Eagle Rock Avenue and left into the park.

Shortly after Newark was settled in 1666 a surveying station was located on Eagle Rock, named for bald eagles that called the rock home. Although the park is undeveloped today it was a busy place through the early 1900s with trolley lines, car races, vacationers and a casino (the non-gambling old-time kind).

The deciduous forest of the 408-acre reservation is striped with bridle trails and footpaths, some marked and some not. The park is most known for its direct views into New York City.

79
Manumuskin River Preserve
Cumberland County

Take Route 55 to Exit 21 onto Schooner Landing Road. Turn left at the stop sign. Follow the road to the gate at the end; the preserve is on the right.

Europeans settled along the 12-mile long Manumuskin River in 1720; remains of chimneys and foundations can be seen along the river trail. The river corridor has remained nearly undisturbed under a rich forest canopy producing superb water quality for nine miles from its headwaters in Atlantic County until it encounters tides from the Delaware Bay. The pure water supports a host of threatened New Jersey species, most notably a population of sensitive joint vetch. This member of the bean family is found nowhere else in the state and the stand here is the largest and healthiest in the world.

The preserve started in 1983 with a donation of 6.65 acres - a couple of big backyards. Today it covers more than 3,500 acres, the largest Nature Conservancy in New Jersey. Dogs are typically not permitted on conservancy lands but they can hike on the bridle trails here.

80
Delaware and Raritan Canal State Park
Mercer and Somerset counties
The canal towpath can be accessed many places; the canal office is at 145 Mapleton Road in Princeton.

When canal building fever swept America in the early 1800s it didn't take much imagination to dream of a water route between New York and Philadelphia across central New Jersey. Ships could navigate up the Delaware River to Bordentown and to New Brunswick in the east so all that was required was to dig a ditch between the two villages. Construction began in 1830 and by 1834 the canal was open. The main artery - 75 feet wide and seven feet deep and all hand dug - stretched 44 miles and another feeder line ran down the Delaware River to Trenton for 22 miles.

The Delaware and Raritan was one of America's busiest canals and staved off competition from the railroads at a profit until almost 1900. It remained open until 1932 until the last coal barge was grounded. The State of New Jersey took over the property as a water supply system and today the canal remains virtually intact. The state park is a 70-mile linear park connecting fields and forests along its route.

Canine hiking along the old towpath uses natural and crushed gravel surfaces. Several mill buildings, wooden bridges and canal structures are reminders of the bustling times that were once routine here. The canal still brims with activity today - almost any time you can count on sharing the trail with joggers, fishermen, cyclists, horseback riders - and other dogs.

81
Merrill Creek Reservoir

Warren County

Route 57 to Mountain Road to Richline Road to Merrill Creek Road

Since it opened in 1989 Merrill Creek Reservoir has become a popular destination for wildlife enthusiasts. The resevoir was built to store water for release into the Delaware River during periods of low flow. When the river is high, water flows back to the reservoir through a 3.5-mile pipe.

An exceptionally attractive trail system runs through a plump peninsula on the eastern side of the lake. There is open space aplenty and airy woodlands, including a pine plantation. The black-marked *Perimeter Trail* sweeps around the water for 5.5 miles, mostly on old farm roads. Except for a steep grade here and there and a rocky patch or two this is easy walking for your dog.

If you are the type who likes to let your dog off the leash when no one is around, Merrill Creek Reservoir is not the place for you. A sign warns that anyone seen with a dog off the leash will be escorted off the property and forever banned.

82
Deer Path Park

Hunterdon County

The park is located between Flemington and Clinton on Route 31. Exit onto Woodschurch Road and follow the signs to the park.

The canine hiker at Deer Park will find a pleasing blend of meadow and woods walking and level hiking and climbing. The main attraction will be across Woodschurch Road, a 600-foot knob that exploded into existence in a volcanic eruption during the Triassic Period. After some cuppy going on horse trails through old farm fields (look for a natural fence of gnarled osage orange trees), the figure-eight *Nature Trail* heads up the verdant hillside. The entire path is 1.5 miles back to the trailhead but the *Peter Buell Trail* branches off the main trail to cross Round Mountain on its wasy to a different trailhead/parking lot.

The recreational section of Deer Path Park should not be overlooked if it is not a busy day. This old farm, and later summer camp, is surrounded by two miles of open cross-country trails that are especially palatable to your dog on a sunny day.

83
South Branch Reservation

Hunterdon County

To Echo Hill Environmental Education Area, take Route 31 north of Flemington 5.6 miles from circle. Make a right onto the jug handle for Stanton Station Road. Travel .4 mile to Lilac Drive and turn right to park entrance.

The South Branch of the Raritan River drains over 1,100 miles - more than any river in New Jersey. The South Branch Reservation is a pack of twelve parks and preserves that highlight the historic and natural delights along the river. A good way to spend a day with your dog is to drive through the watershed in Hunterdon County, stopping at the various sections and enjoying a short hike or swim.

Clumped together, the dozen parks total more than 1,000 acres. Several are old farms and offer pleasant open-field canine hiking; others serve up wooded trails. At Echo Hill, home of the South Branch Watershed Association, the Civilian Conservation Corps cut down the original orchard and blanketed the property with 200,000 evergreens in 1939. A journey down the South Branch is a wonderful education in bridge engineering with the river crossed by stone arch bridges, iron truss bridges and pier-and-deck spans.

And sometimes when you'd get up in the middle of the night you'd hear the reassuring thump, thump of her tail on the floor, letting you know that she was there and thinking of you.
-William Cole

84
Washington Valley Park

Somerset County

From I-78 take Exit 33 for Route 525, heading south. Go 3.1 miles to Washington Valley Road. Turn left and go to Vosseler Avenue and make a right on Miller Road to the park OR turn right on Washington Valley Road and make a quick left onto Newman's Lane to the parking area on left.

Washington Valley Park offers two park areas. The Miller Road parking lot leads to a Hawk Watch overlook that is one of the East Coast's premier locations to watch raptors migrate south each fall. The canine hiking here is rugged - both on the hills and on the paws across rocky trails. With more than seven miles of trails in Washington Valley Park, it is best to leave this yellow-blazed trail system to the mountain bikers who frequent the park.

Newman's Lane is the jumping off point for three different trail systems, two that run on either side of the picturesque Washington Valley Reservoir. Your dog can spend hours touring these pine and hemlock forests between the First and Second Watchung Mountains. Hopefully, you'll be able to get a trail map to decipher the trails in this spread-out 715-acre park; if not there is a mapboard to study at Newman's Lane.

85
Monmouth Battlefield State Park

Monmouth County

From the Garden State Parkway, take Exit 123 to Route 9 South for 15 miles to business Route 33 West. Park is located 1.5 miles on the right.

The American Army came of age in 1778 in the Battle of Monmouth, forcing the British from the field in a brilliant counterattack led by George Washington. The General had planned a support role for himself, hoping to deliver a final, fatal blow to the British Army but when he started for the battle he instead discovered 5,000 of his best troops in a confused retreat. A stunned Washington immediately took personal command from Charels Lee, the general he had entrusted the attack to, and stopped the retreat. Eagerly his troops, hardened from their experience at Valley Forge, rallied to rout the British in record June heat. It was the last major battle of the Revolution in the north and Washington's finest hour in the field.

Trails, unadorned with historical markers, traverse the scene of some of the most desperate fighting. Most of the canine hiking in the historical park is across open fields with plenty of soft grass for your dog's travels.

86
Branch Brook Park
Essex County
In downtown Newark; I-280 to Exit 15 and north on Bloomfield to park.

This four-mile linear park, a block or two wide for most of its length, became the first county park in the United States when it was authorized in 1895. It was conceived as a natural space in a valley of a brook flowing into the Passaic River known as Old Blue Jay Swamp but additional land donations and gifts transformed the open space into a recognizable park of lakes, flower gardens, and ballfields.

Expect easy canine hiking on paved paths and dirt scars across grassy lawns and patchy woodlands. The highlight at Branch Brook Park each year is the flowering of more than 2,000 dogwood trees during April. The cherry trees in Newark are more numerous and more varied than the famous cherry trees in Washington, D.C.

87
Great Falls of the Passiac River
Passaic County
From I-80 take Exit 57 B-A. Follow signs for "Downtown Paterson" and make the 1st left onto Cianci Street. Go one light to Market Street and turn left. Market Street ends at Spruce Street. Turn right onto Spruce Street. Go one block to McBride Avenue Extension and turn right. The Great Falls parking area is on the right.

This is certainly not a vigorous hike, more of an interesting place to walk your dog. The thundering Great Falls roar over a 280-foot crest, plunging 77 feet with more water volume than any Eastern waterfall not named Niagara. Two hundred million years ago hot magma erupted from the earth and cooled to become the basaltic First Watchung Ridge, oblivious to erosion. The trapped Passaic River began poking around for a way around the ridge and finally found it here.

Alexander Hamilton was the first to link the power of the Falls to industry after dining at its base during the Revolutionary War. His vision of a great industrial city here was not quite realized but over the years the water turned machines for textiles, steam locomotices, revolvers and other paterson industries.

The Great Falls can be viewed from Overlook Park and Hamilton Park on either side of the river. You walk your dog across the chasm between the two parks on the eighth bridge built at the Falls.

88
Hammonton Lake Natural Area

Burlington County

In the Pinelands town of Hammonton at North Egg Habor Road and Park Avenue.

During the War of 1812, William Coffin built a sawmill along what later became known as Hammonton Lake. Upon his death, his sons John Hammond Coffin and Edward Winslow Coffin inherited the factory and the settlement became known as "Hammondton." The lake is now the centerpiece of an attractive park.

The Natural Area is a wooded area next to the park, a duck-billed peninsula surrounded by the lake on three sides. For canine hikers who want a taste of   the pinelands without the vast forests this is a pleasant option. An unclean Hammonton Lake has been closed to swimmers at times in recent years but that won't stop your dog from a refershing dip.

89
Lincoln Park

Hudson County

Lincoln Park is divided into Lincoln Park East and Lincoln Park West in Jersey City; the East Park entrance is at Kennedy Boulevard and Belmont Avenue.

Hudson County has seven parks and Lincoln Park, in Jersey City, is the largest. It is notable for a restored 53-foot fountain decorated with spouting frogs and allegorical figures, designed by Pierre J. Cheron in 1911, and a 20-foot statue of a seated, Abraham Lincoln, designed by James Earle Fraser, best remembered for his design of the buffalo nickel. The park grounds were laid out by landscape architects Daniel W. Langton and Charles N. Lowrie in 1907.

Lincoln Park is a good choice to show your dog a classic urban park with promenades and gazebos and large grassy spaces suitable for a game of fetch. Walking paths set you off on a canine hike around the perimeter of the 273-acre city park.

90
Penn State Forest
Burlington County
Take Route 563 to Lake Oswego Road in Jenkins Neck, and follow for three miles.

You say you've already taken your dog to Wharton State Forest and saw one person a four-hour hike and thought your dog was feeling a little crowded? Try Penn State Forest, over to the east a ways. You will still be in the Pine Barrens, the largest contiguous swath of greenspace between Boston and Washington. There are over 3,000 undeveloped acres in Penn State Forest; most canine hikers start their explorations at Lake Oswego that sports a picnic and canoe-launch site. Canine hiking is down unmarked sand roads.

The highlight of Penn State Forest is its Pygmy Pine Forest in an area known as the Plains. The trees rarely grow over four feet and you may mistake this for a young forest but these survivors have been trying to suck sustenance out of the sandy, acidic soil for decades. No one knows why the trees don't grow but theories center on the active fire cycle in the Pine Barrens, where on average a fire occurs every day of the year.

91
Dorbrook Recreation Area
Monmouth County
Take the Garden State Parkway to Exit 109 and head west on Route 520, New-man Springs Road. Turn left on Swimming River Road and right on Route 537 to park.

The first land for this park was acquired from the estate of Murray Rosenberg, creator of Miles Shore stores. Later additions included Festoon Farm, a horse spread named for the English import, Festoon, who won the One Thousand Guinea Stakes at Newcastle, first contested in 1814.

As active recreation areas go for hiking with your dog, this is one of the best. The park is big at 535 acres and there is plenty of room for 2.4 miles of paved trail on two loops. This is very easy going and with its flat terrain has been named the best place in Monmouth County for rollerbladers so watch out from behind.

92
Loantaka Brook Reservation
Morris County

From I-287 take Exit 35 onto Madison Avenue and head east. Turn left on South Street to park on left.

There are nearly five miles of trails in this narrow neck of a park but this is not the place to come to lose yourself in nature with your dog. The genesis of the park is from the Seaton Hackney Farm and the stables are a dominant feature of today's activities.

The canine hiking is easy and you have your choice of curvy, paved paths or bridle paths winding through light forest and wetlands. The flat terrain brings out the inline skaters and strollers to roll alongside the horses.

93
Thompson Park
Monmouth County

The park is on Route 520 (Newman Springs Road) in Lincroft. From the Garden State Parkway Southbond turn right; Northbound turn left.

The centerpiece of Brookdale Farm, a 32-room Colonial revival mansion built in 1896 by Lewis and Geraldine Thompson, was ravaged by fire in February 2006 forever altering the character of this park. You can still bring your dog to this beautiful former thoroughbred farm to tour old roads and exercise trails. A paved jogging path trips the length of the park for 1.8 miles in open fields and tickles woodlands.

In the western section of the park your dog can enjoy an off-leash area. You can reach it by using the maintenance entrance.

"Do not make the mistake of treating your dogs like humans or they will treat you like dogs."
-Martha Scott

94
North Brigantine Natural Area
Atlantic County
Take Route 30 into Atlantic City from Route 9 and head north on Brigantine Boulevard through the town of Brigantine all the way to the end.

It may change due to concerns about nesting plovers but this undeveloped area at the northern tip of Brigantine is open to dogs. You can hike north on the shore, ducking out of the way of surf fishermen, and take the hook along the inlet and head back. If the Atlantic waves are too intimidating for your dog, the gentle surf of the bay will be a perfect place to swim. This entire hike up and back - completely on sand - will take about an hour if you keep moving and don't linger for too many swims.

95
Westcott Nature Preserve
Hunterdon County
Take Route 29 North along the Delaware River to Route 519, past Stockton. In Rosemont make a left onRaven Rock-Rosemont Road to the park.

While less than a mile long there is plenty for your dog to experience on this loop that makes it a worthy detour when traveling along the Delaware River. This easy canine hike begins and ends in an open meadow that abuts a diverse woodland of red maple, oak, ash - and hemlock. Along the lively Lockatong Creek, in terrain too difficult for loggers to negotiate, grows a magnificent stand of hemlock. Although the trail works atop the creek there is an opportunity for your dog to climb down and enjoy the spa-like rapids.

96
Timber Creek Park
Gloucester County
On the southeast corner of Hurffville Road (Route 41) and Cooper Street/Almonesson Road.

This small park offers an eyehook trail whose highlight is a view of the wetlands of the Big Timber Creek estuary, home to ducks, geese, herons and kingfishers. The wide, soft dirt and sand trails follow a rolling, wooded path along the slopes above the marsh. This pleasant stroll takes less than one half hour but there is more at the Old Pine Farm (end of Rankin Avenue).

97
Bear Swamp

Burlington County
Hawkins Road off Route 206 south of Route 70.

A labyrinth of unmarked and unmaintained trails provide access to hundreds of protected acres of mixed hardwoods and pine trees. The soft dirt and sand trails are generally wide but there are places that will require bushwhacking and picking your way through muddy low spots. Look for trails leading into the woods on the north side of Hawkins Road, that switches from a macadam to dirt surface in the region of Bear Swamp. One such entrance is on the east side of a small bridge across Little Creek on the western edge of the hard surface/soft surface switchover.

98
Berlin Park

Camden County
Between White Horse Pike, New Freedom Road and Park Drive.

Several miles of densely wooded trails course through the park behind the Environmental Studies Center at the corner of Broad Street and Park Drive. The main pathway through the spine of the park is wide and composed of pebbly sand; it runs alongside the Great Egg Harbor River. Designated a Wild and Scenic River, the Great Egg Harbor is narrow, dark and forboding. Unmarked dirt trails branch from the trunk in narrow slivers through the thick woods. Also available is a short nature loop inside a wired path.

"If your dog is fat, you aren't getting enough exercise."
- Anonymous

99
New Brooklyn Park
Camden County
On New Brooklyn Road north of the Atlantic City Expressway and east of Route 536.

The park is the terminus of the Great Egg Harbor River where it feeds into New Brooklyn Lake. On the north shore of the lake there are unmarked trails and dirt roads in the woods of the 758-acre park. The trails are paw-friendly sand and dirt. A small sand beach offers access to the shallow waters of the 100-acre lake. A paved multi-purpose trail winds through the developed sections of the park.

100
Edwin B. Forsythe National Wildlife Refuge
Atlantic County
Follow Route 72 to Route 9 North. Take Route 9 North to Lower Shore Road. Turn left. At second fork, turn right (Collinstown Road). Continue on road.

The pristine Holgate Unit in the Barnegat Division at the tip of Long Island is the star attraction at the Atlantic seashore refuge but it is off-limits to dogs. But there is still lemonade to be made from the lemons dished out here by the U.S. Fish & Wild-life Service - dogs are welcome to enjoy the nature trails in the Brigantine Division.

There are four short trails that will take you into woodlands and salt marshes along the leisurely eight-mile Wildlife Drive. This is a quiet place to bring your dog for relaxed canine hiking.

Traveling With Your Dog In New Jersey

All veterinary hospitals provide emergency care during business hours; the following offer care after hours:

Sussex County
Newton Veterinary Hospital
116 Hampton House Road
Newton   973-383-4321
open 24 hours

Bergen County
Oradell Animal Hospital
580 Winters Avenue
Paramus   201-262-0010
open 24 hours

Essex County
Animal Emergency/Referral Service
1237 Bloomfield Avenue
Fairfield   973-226-3282
open 24 hours

Morris County
Alliance Emergency Vet Clinic
540 Route 10 West
Randolph   973-328-2844
open nights, weekends, holidays

Middlesex County
Central Jersey Vet Emergency Service
543 Route 27
Iselin   732-283-3535
open nights, weekends, holidays

Somerset County
Animerge
21 Route 205 North
Raritan   908-707-9077
open nights, weekends, holidays

Monmouth County
Red Bank Veterinary Hospital
197 Hance Avenue
Tinton Falls   732-747-3636
open 24 hours

Monmouth County
Veterinary Surgical and Diagnostic
34 Trenton-Clarksburg Road
Clarksburg   609-259-8300
open 24 hours

Monmouth County
Garden State Veterinary Specialists
1 Pine Street
Tinton Falls   732-922-0011
open 24 hours

Ocean County
Jersey Shore Veterinary Emergency
1000 Route 70
Lakewood   732-363-3200
open nights, weekends, holidays

Burlington County
Animal Emergency - South Jersey
220 Moorestown-Mt. Laurel Road
Mt. Laurel   856-234-7626
open nights, weekends, holidays

Atlantic County
South Jersey Vet Emergency Service
535 Maple Avenue
Linwood   609-926-5300
open 24 hours

Your Dog At The Beach

It is hard to imagine many places a dog is happier than at a beach. Whether running around on the sand, jumping in the water or just lying in the sun, every dog deserves a day at the beach. But all too often dog owners stopping at a sandy stretch of beach are met with signs designed to make hearts - human and canine alike - droop: NO DOGS ON BEACH. Below are rules for taking your dog on a day trip to one of our Atlantic Ocean beaches.

Asbury Park	Dogs are allowed on the beach in off-season
Atlantic City	Dogs are not permitted on the beaches or boardwalk anytime
Avalon	Dogs are not permitted on the beach, boardwalk or dunes between March 1 and September 30
Avon-By-The-Sea	Dogs allowed on beach from November 1 to April 1 but never on the boardwalk
Barnegat Light	Dogs are prohibited from May 1 to October 1
Beach Haven	No dogs allowed on the beach
Belmar	Dogs are not allowed on the beach year-round
Bradley Beach	Dogs are allowed from October 15 to April 15
Brigantine	Dogs are allowed on the beach from 14th Street north to the northernmost jetty

Cape May	Dogs are not allowed on the beach, boardwalk or outdoor shopping areas any time
Cape May Point	No dogs allowed on the beach
Gateway National Recreation Area - Sandy Hook	Dogs allowed on the beach from Labor Day to March 15

You never know what treasure will wash ashore on a beach,
like this coconut at Gateway National Recreation Area.

Island Beach State Park	Dogs are not allowed in recreational areas but have access to other beaches any time of the year
Lavallette	No dogs allowed on beach but can go on boardwalk after Labor Day
Mantoloking	Dogs allowed on the beach October 1 to May 15 anytime; otherwise dogs allowed from sunrise to 8 AM and 6 PM to sunset
North Wildwood	Dogs are not allowed on the beach from May 15 to September 15

Ocean City	Dogs are never allowed on the boardwalk but can be leashed on the beach from October 1 to April 30
Ocean Grove	Dogs are permitted on the beach and boardwalk from October 1 to May 1
Point Pleasant	Dogs are allowed anytime from September 15 until June 15; before 8:00 AM and after 6:00 PM in the summer
Sea Isle City	No dogs are permitted on the beach, beach approaches or promenade at any time
Ship Bottom	No dogs allowed on the beach until October 1
Spring Lake	Dogs are allowed on the beach in the off-season
Stone Harbor	No dogs allowed on the beach, boardwalk or dunes anytime between March 1 and September 30
Surf City	No dogs allowed on the beach
Wildwood	No dogs allowed on the beach
Wildwood Crest	No animals of any kind allowed on the beach

Tips For Taking Your Dog To The Beach

- The majority of dogs can swim and love it, but dogs entering the water for the first time should be tested; never throw a dog into the water. Start in shallow water and call your dog's name - or try to coax him in with a treat or toy. Always keep your dog within reach.

- Another way to introduce your dog to the water is with a dog that already swims and is friendly with your dog. Let your dog follow his friend.

- If your dog begins to doggie paddle with his front legs only, lift his hind legs and help him float. He should quickly catch on and will keep his back end up.

- Swimming is a great form of exercise, but don't let your dog overdo it. He will be using new muscles and may tire quickly.

- Be careful of strong tides that are hazardous for even the best swimmers.

- Cool ocean water is tempting to your dog. Do not allow him to drink too much sea water. Salt in the water will make him sick. Salt and other minerals found in the ocean can damage your dog's coat so regular bathing is essential.

- Check with a lifeguard for daily water conditions - dogs are easy targets for jellyfish and sea lice.

- Dogs can get sunburned, especially short-haired dogs and ones with pink skin and white hair. Limit your dog's exposure when the sun is strong and apply sunblock to his ears and nose 30 minutes before going outside.

- If your dog is out of shape, don't encourage him to run on the sand, which is strenuous exercise and a dog that is out of shape can easily pull a tendon or ligament.

As a young lawyer, 19th century Senator George Graham Vest of Missouri, addressed the jury on behalf of his client, suing a neighbor who had killed his dog. Vest's speech has come to be known as "Tribute to the Dog."

The best friend a man has in the world may turn against him and become his enemy. His son or daughter that he has reared with loving care may prove ungrateful. Those who are nearest and dearest to us, those whom we trust with our happiness and our good name may become traitors to their faith. The money that a man has, he may lose. It flies away from him, perhaps when he needs it most. A man's reputation may be sacrificed in a moment of ill-considered action. The people who are prone to fall on their knees to do us honor when success is with us may be the first to throw the stone of malice when failure settles its cloud upon our heads. The one absolutely unselfish friend that man can have in this selfish world, the one that never deserts him, the one that never proves ungrateful or treacherous is his dog. A man's dog stands by him in prosperity and in poverty, in health and in sickness. He will sleep on the cold ground, where the wintry winds blow and the snow drives fiercely, if only he may be near his master's side. He will kiss the hand that has no food to offer; he will lick the wounds and sores that come in an encounter with the roughness of the world. He guards the sleep of his pauper master as if he were a prince. When all other friends desert, he remains. When riches take wings, and reputation falls to pieces, he is as constant in his love as the sun in its journey through the heavens. If fortune drives the master forth an outcast in the world, friendless and homeless, the faithful dog asks no higher privilege than that of accompanying him, to guard him against danger, to fight against his enemies. And when the last scene of all comes, and death takes his master in its embrace and his body is laid away in the cold ground, no matter if all other friends pursue their way, there by the graveside will the noble dog be found, his head between his paws, his eyes sad, but open in alert watchfulness, faithful and true even in death.

Index To Parks

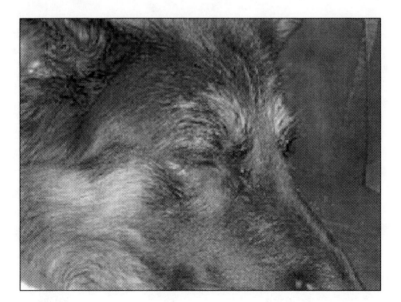

Printed in the United States
64692LVS00002B/103-141